Handel

by

Edward J. Dent

Handel
by Edward J. Dent

ISBN: 978-93-62207-00-5

Published by

DOUBLE 9 BOOKS

2/13-B, Ansari Road
Daryaganj, New Delhi – 110002
info@double9books.com
www.double9books.com
Tel. 011-40042856

ABOUT THE AUTHOR

Edward Joseph Dent FBA, also known as Edward J. Dent, was an English musicologist, teacher, translator, and critic. Dent, a significant figure in musicology and criticism, was Professor of Music at the University of Cambridge from 1926 to 1941. Dent was born at Ribston, Yorkshire, the son of John Dent, a landowner and politician. He was educated at Bilston Grange and Eton, where he studied music under Charles Harford Lloyd. He enrolled at King's College, Cambridge, in 1895, earning a B.A. in Classical Tripos in 1898, a Mus.B. in 1899 after studying under Charles Wood and Charles Villiers Stanford, and an M.A. in 1902. In March 1902, he was elected a Fellow of his institution after achieving distinction in music as both a researcher and a composer. Dent was Professor of Music at Cambridge University from 1926 to 1941, when he taught Arthur Bliss, Arnold Cooke, and Cecil Armstrong Gibbs. He served as President of the International Society of Composers and Musicians from 1922 to 1938, as well as the International Music Society from 1931 to 1949. He was the governor of Sadler's Wells Opera and translated numerous libretti for it. He wrote notable publications about Alessandro Scarlatti, Ferruccio Busoni, Handel, English operas, and Mozart's operas.

CONTENTS

CHRONOLOGY

1685.... *Birth at Halle.*

1702.... *Entered University; organist of the Cathedral.*

1703.... *Went to Hamburg.*

1705.... *First opera: Almira (Hamburg).*

1707.... *Arrival in Italy.*

1710.... *Appointment at Hanover; first visit to London.*

1711.... *First London opera: Rinaldo.*

1712.... *Second visit to London.*

1717.... *Appointment to the Duke of Chandos.*

1720.... *Opening of Royal Academy of Music (Opera).*

1726.... *Naturalized as a British subject.*

1728.... *The Beggar's Opera. Collapse of the Academy.*

1732.... *First public oratorio: Esther.*

1733.... *Festival at Oxford.*

1737.... *Collapse of Opera; Handel bankrupt and paralysed.*

1741.... *Last opera: Deidamia.*

1742.... *Messiah at Dublin.*

1751.... *First signs of blindness. Last oratorio Jeptha.*

1759.... *Death in London.*

CHAPTER I

The name of Handel suggests to most people the sound of music unsurpassed in massiveness and dignity, and the familiar portraits of the composer present us with a man whose external appearance was no less massive and dignified than his music. Countless anecdotes point him out to us as a well-known figure in the life of London during the reigns of Queen Anne and the first two Georges. He lies buried in Westminster Abbey. One would expect every detail of his life to be known and recorded, his every private thought to be revealed with the pellucid clarity of his immortal strains. It is not so; to assemble the bare facts of Handel's life is a problem which has baffled the most laborious of his biographers, and his inward personality is more mysterious than that of any other great musician of the last two centuries.

The *Memoirs of the Life of the late George Frederic Handel*, written by the Rev. John Mainwaring in 1760, a year after his death, is the first example of a whole book devoted to the biography of a musician. The author had never known Handel himself; he obtained his material chiefly from Handel's secretary, John Christopher Smith the younger. Mainwaring is our only authority for the story of Handel's early life. Many of his statements have been proved to be untrue, but there is undoubtedly a foundation of truth beneath most of them, however misleading either Smith's memory or Mainwaring's imagination may have been. The rest of our knowledge has to be built up from scattered documents of various kinds, helped out by the reminiscences of Dr. Burney and Sir John Hawkins. For the inner life of Mozart and Beethoven we can turn to copious letters and other personal writings; Handel's extant letters do not amount to more than about twenty in all, and it is only rarely that they throw much light on the workings of his mind.

The family of Handel belonged originally to Breslau. The name is found in various forms; it seems originally to have been *Händeler* signifying trader, but by the time the composer was born the spelling *Händel* had been adopted. This is the correct German form of his name; in Italy he wrote his name *Hendel*, in order to ensure its proper pronunciation, and in England he was known, for the same reason, as Handel. The Handels of Breslau had for several generations been coppersmiths. Valentine Handel, the composer's grandfather, born in 1582, migrated to Halle, where two of his sons followed the same trade. His third son, George, born 1622, became a barber-surgeon. At the age of twenty he married the widow of the barber to whom he had been apprenticed; she was twelve years older than he was. In 1682 she died, and George Handel, although sixty years of age, married a second wife within half a year. Her name was Dorothea Taust; her father, like most of his ancestors, was a clergyman. Her age was thirty-two. Her first child, born in 1684, died at birth; her second, born February 23, 1685, was baptised the following day with the name of George Frederic.

The town of Halle had originally belonged to the Dukes of Saxony, but after the Thirty Years' War it was assigned to the Elector of Brandenburg. George Frederic Handel was therefore born a Prussian. But Duke Augustus of Saxony was allowed to keep his court at the Moritzburg in Halle, and it was this prince who made George Handel his personal surgeon. After Duke Augustus's death in 1680, Halle was definitely transferred to Brandenburg, and the new Duke, Johann Adolf, took up his residence at Weissenfels, twenty-five miles to the south-west of Halle. At the time of George Frederic's birth, Halle had relapsed into being a quiet provincial town. The musical life of Germany in those days was chiefly centred in the numerous small courts, each of which did its best to imitate the magnificence of Louis XIV at Paris and Versailles. But the seventeenth century, although it produced very few musicians of outstanding greatness, was a century of restless musical activity throughout Europe, especially in the more private and domestic branches of the art. The Reformation had made music the vehicle of personal devotion, and the enormous output of a peculiarly intimate type of sacred music, both in Germany and in England, shows that there must have been a keen demand for it in Protestant home life.

George Handel, the surgeon, seems to have hated music. There is no evidence that either his wife or her sister, who shared their home after her father's death in 1685, was musically gifted, but the mere fact of their being the daughters of a Lutheran pastor makes it probable that they had had some education in the art. We may safely guess that the composer inherited his musical talents from the Taust family. He showed his inclination for music at a very early age, with such insistence indeed that his father forbade him to touch any musical instrument. There is a well-known story of his contriving to smuggle a clavichord into a garret without his father's knowledge in order to practise on it while the rest of the family were asleep, but for this tale Mainwaring is our only authority. It is very probable that old Handel was irritated by the sound of his son's early efforts and regarded music as a waste of time; his wife may perhaps have encouraged the child's obvious abilities, taking care that he made music only in some part of the house where he would not disturb his father.

At the age of seven he was sent to the Lutheran Grammar School, and he may very likely have had some instruction in singing while there. In any case there can be no doubt that he was taught more than the mere rudiments of music in childhood, however severe his father's opposition may have been. He was between seven and nine when his father took him to Weissenfels, where he was required to attend on the Duke. It is quite probable that the child may have been taken there several times, especially as a relative of his was in regular service in the Duke's establishment. One day he was allowed to play on the organ in the palace chapel; the Duke happened to hear him, made enquiries as to who the player was, and at once urged on the father the duty of having him properly trained for a musical career.

Old Handel remained obstinate; he was determined that his son should have a liberal education and become a lawyer. By his own efforts he had raised himself to a position of some distinction and affluence; it was only natural that he should wish his son to enter on life with better advantages than he himself had enjoyed. He at any rate followed the advice of the Duke so far as to place the boy under the musical tuition of Friedrich Zachow, the organist of the Lutheran church at Halle.

The next episode in George Frederic's career has considerably puzzled his biographers. Mainwaring asserts that in 1698 he went to Berlin, where he was presented to the Electress Sophia Charlotte and made the acquaintance of Ariosti and Giovanni Battista Buononcini, two famous Italian opera composers whom he was to encounter again, in London, many years later. But it is known that Ariosti did not arrive in Berlin until the spring of 1697, and Buononcini not until 1702. And as old Handel died in February 1697, his son cannot have been in Berlin later than about the end of 1696, if it is true (as Mainwaring says) that the Elector offered to send him to Italy, an offer which the father firmly refused to accept for him. If, on the other hand, Mainwaring is right in saying that young Handel went to Berlin with a view to obtaining a musical post there, it is hardly likely that he should have made the journey at ten years of age, and while his father was still living. It seems much more probable that if he ever did visit Berlin it was when he was of an age to form his own judgments as to his future career.

Three days before his seventeenth birthday he matriculated as a law student of the University of Halle, but music must have been the chief occupation of his time. The composer Telemann, four years his senior, spoke of him as being already a musician of importance at Halle when he first met him there, probably in 1700. In March 1702 he was appointed organist at the Cathedral, although he belonged to the Lutheran Church, whereas the Cathedral was Calvinist; considerable scandal had been caused by the intemperance of the Cathedral organist, one Leporin, who was finally dismissed. That Handel should have been given the post at so early an age points to his ability and trustworthiness of character; it also suggests that efficient organists were rare among the Calvinist musicians.

Mainwaring unjustly credited Zachow with Leporin's love of a cheerful glass, and other biographers have perhaps for this reason greatly underrated Zachow's musicianship. Zachow cannot indeed be classed as a great composer, but he was considerably more than merely a sound average teacher. For one thing, he possessed a large library of music. Handel was not only made to master the arts of counterpoint and fugue, but he was also set to study the works of other composers, and to train his sense of style by writing music in direct imitation of them. In those days there was no possibility of buying all sorts of music ready printed. Printing was expensive, and generally clumsy in execution as well; most music was copied by hand, and a musician who wished to acquire a library of music generally did so by borrowing it and copying it. Zachow employed Handel to copy music for him, and no doubt he copied a great deal for himself. Although the opportunities for hearing music would not be very liberal in a town like Halle, Handel, under Zachow, became a well-read musician as well as an accomplished one.

During the seventeenth century the chief contribution of Germany to the art of music was religious, just as the German hymns were her chief contribution to poetry. In Italy, on the other hand, sacred music was of minor importance as compared with the development of opera. But in all music Italy led the way, and German sacred music was constantly influenced by the Italians, with the result that Italian dramatic methods were often used by German composers of sacred music, not with any loss of seriousness and dignity to its character, but rather to the intenser expression of that deep personal religious feeling which characterised both the poetry and the music of the Protestant nations.

Zachow was well acquainted with the Italian masters, and his own Church music shows a vivid dramatic sense; it is easy to see how much Handel learned from him. But although Church cantatas and organ music may have sufficed for the majority of the innumerable worthy German musicians of those days, the form of music which excited the curiosity and interest of the livelier spirits was certainly opera. By 1700, opera had established itself all over Italy, supported mainly by the great princes, but at Venice maintained on a commercial basis by the citizens themselves since

1637. The first attempt at a German opera was made by Heinrich Schütz, at Torgau, ten years earlier. Vienna introduced Italian opera in 1631, and, generally speaking, the Catholic princes of Germany, who one after another followed the example of Vienna, preferred opera in Italian. Protestant Germany inclined more to opera in its own language, though towards the end of the century Italian gradually gained the upper hand at the more important courts. Native German opera owed its origin partly to the visit of the English comedians early in the century, and partly to the musical plays acted by school-boys; from the English "jigs" came the use of short popular songs, and from the school plays the tendency of the early German operas to be of a more or less sacred or edifying character.

Handel's friend, the composer Telemann, tells us that it was not unusual for students from the University of Leipzig to go to Berlin to hear the Italian opera, which had been established by the Electress Sophia Charlotte in 1700, and this suggests that Handel's visit to Berlin may have taken place in 1703 rather than in his childhood. But he certainly had opportunities for seeing operas nearer home. There had been many German operas performed at Halle itself during the twenty years before Handel's birth, and Duke Johann Adolf opened an opera-house at Weissenfels in 1685, in which Philipp Krieger produced German operas regularly for the next thirty years. There was thus every reason for young Handel's growing ambitious to become a composer for the stage, although we have no evidence of his having ever attempted dramatic composition until he left Halle in 1703.

The most important of all the north German opera-houses was that of Hamburg, where the opera did not depend on the patronage of a court, but was organised, as at Venice, as a public entertainment. Hamburg had attempted German opera as early as 1648, and it is interesting to note that the English composer William Brade was one of those who provided the music; but the real history of the Hamburg opera may be said to begin with the performance of Theile's *Adam and Eve* in the newly built theatre in the Goose-Market in 1678. When Handel arrived in Hamburg in the summer of 1703 the biblical operas had long come to an end, and the theatre was under the management of Reinhold Keiser.

Keiser was a musician of remarkable genius. His father was a disreputable organist, and his mother a young lady of noble family who had been hastily married at the age of sixteen. Born near Weissenfels in 1674, he had begun his operatic career at Brunswick at the age of eighteen; three years later he took over the direction of the opera at Hamburg, where he produced a large number of operas composed by himself. As a composer, Keiser had a singular fluency of melody in a style that hovers between those of Germany and Italy; had he been a man of more solid character he might have accomplished greater things. But he had inherited from his parents a love of pleasure and debauchery; extravagant in his private life, he was no less extravagant in his theatrical management, and was ready to provide his audiences with anything in the way of startling sensation. One of his most famous operas was on the subject of Störtebeker, a notorious highwayman (1704), in which murders were represented with the most disgusting realism.

Hamburg was the Venice of the north and, like Venice, a city of pleasure; but its pleasures were often of a coarse and licentious description. Life in Hamburg was probably not much unlike that of Restoration London; but though Keiser may well be set beside Purcell, Hamburg had no dramatists to compare with Congreve, hardly even with Shadwell. Jeremy Collier, however, was far outdone in vituperation by the puritan clergy who, not altogether without reason, castigated the immorality of the Hamburg stage.

Handel seems to have arrived in Hamburg in early summer of 1703, for we first hear of him there on July 2, when he met Johann Mattheson in the church of St. Mary Magdalen. It seems to have been a chance acquaintance, to judge from Mattheson's account; it stuck in Mattheson's memory for many years and he remembered especially the pastry-cook's boy who blew the organ for Handel and himself. Mattheson was four years older than Handel; he was one of those precociously gifted, versatile, attractive, and rather vain young men who are endowed with so many talents that they never achieve distinction in any branch of art. He is remembered now only by the literary work of his later life, in which he shows himself as a voluminous pedant and an embittered critic. He made friends with Handel on the spot, and took him under his own protection, providing him with almost daily free meals at his father's house. He evidently regarded him as a very simple and provincial young musician, a notable organist indeed, and a master of such learned devices as counterpoint and fugue, but a dull composer, turning out endless arias and cantatas with no sense of the fashionable Italian taste.

It was Mattheson, by his own account, who introduced Handel to the musical life of Hamburg. The opera was closed for the summer, and Keiser's celebrated winter concerts, at which the wealthy society of Hamburg listened to the most famous singers and regaled themselves with tokay, had not yet begun; but there was no lack of social distractions, in which music no doubt played its part. In August the two friends made a journey to Lubeck, to compete for the post of organist at the Marienkirche in succession to Dietrich Buxtehude, who was nearly seventy and ready to retire. But both Buxtehude and the town council insisted that the new organist should marry his predecessor's daughter, in order to save the town the necessity of providing for her; she was considerably older than the two youthful candidates, and they both withdrew in haste. Late in life Mattheson married the daughter of an English clergyman; Handel remained a bachelor to the end of his days.

It was no doubt through Mattheson that Handel, in the autumn, entered the opera band as a humble second violinist. He seems to have been of a very retiring and quiet disposition, although of a dry humour. Opera management at Hamburg was no less precarious than it was in London; Keiser could not afford the Italian singers patronised by the German princes, and his performances had often to be helped out by amateurs of all classes. On one occasion the harpsichord-player failed him; Handel took his place at short notice, and his musicianship was at once recognised. Unfortunately Mattheson, whose chronology is always rather uncertain, does not tell us when this occurred. In addition to his duties in the orchestra, Handel earned a living by teaching private pupils, and through Mattheson he was engaged by Mr. John Wyche, the English Envoy, as music-master to his small son Cyril.

Early in 1704 Mattheson went to Holland, where he had some success in organising concerts at Amsterdam, and was offered the post of organist at Haarlem. He seems to have had some idea of seeking his fortune in England; he spoke English well, and may have had useful connexions in England through Mr. John Wyche. But in March Handel wrote to him that the Hamburg opera could not get on without him, and to Hamburg he returned. It soon must have become clear to him that Handel was rapidly outgrowing any need of his condescending patronage. A *Passion according to St. John*, the words of which had been written by Postel, an opera-poet turned pietist, had been set to music by Handel, and performed on Good Friday with marked success. Mattheson arrived too late to hear it, but it is significant that twenty years later he published a scathing criticism of it, although it is a work of little importance in relation to Handel's complete career, and can seldom have been performed. A Passion oratorio by Keiser was produced at the same time, it may well have been that Handel's work, youthful and conventional as it is, was enough to arouse the jealousy of both Keiser and Mattheson.

Shortly after Easter, Keiser began the composition of a new opera, *Almira*, on a libretto by the local poet Feustking, but for some reason or other he found it necessary to call in Handel's assistance, and eventually left the whole work to Handel to compose. It was to be produced in the autumn. Handel seems to have consulted Mattheson over every detail of the opera; there exists a complete score in Mattheson's handwriting, with corrections and additions by Handel. Mattheson spent the summer enjoying a country holiday in Mecklenburg; Handel probably went on with his opera, at Hamburg. In October, just as the opera season was reopening, Mattheson contrived to get himself engaged by Sir Cyril Wych as tutor to his son; he also took over the boy's musical education, hinting that Handel was dismissed for neglect of his duties. In view of Handel's strictly honourable character it is difficult to believe that he was guilty of neglect, and we may naturally suppose him to have resented the loss of a lucrative appointment.

The first opera of the autumn was not Handel's *Almira*, but an opera by Mattheson, called *Cleopatra*. Mattheson, always eager to exhibit his versatility, sang the part of Antony himself, and, not content with that, came into the orchestra as soon as Antony had died on the stage and kept himself in view of the audience by conducting at the harpsichord. For several performances Handel made no objection and gave up his seat to Mattheson when the moment came, but on December 5, for some reason or other, he refused, to the surprise and indignation of the composer. German musicians in those days were a quarrelsome crew; at the court of Stuttgart the musicians were so much given to knocking each other on the head with their instruments, even in the august presence of His Serene Highness, that there was hardly one left undamaged. It was only to be expected that the friends of Handel and Mattheson should egg them on to fight a duel in the street; luckily Mattheson's sword broke on a button of Handel's coat, and the duel ended. On December 30 a town councillor effected a reconciliation; the rivals dined together at Mattheson's house and went on to the rehearsal of *Almira*, which was brought out on January 8, 1705, with Mattheson as the principal tenor.

Almira, the libretto of which was partly in German and partly in Italian, ran continuously for about twenty performances until February 25, when it was succeeded by *Nero*, another opera which Handel had hastily composed for the occasion. *Nero*, in which Mattheson sang the title part, was a failure. The music is lost, but the libretto survives, and that is enough to account for the collapse. The opera had three performances only. In the very same season Keiser re-set *Nero* to music himself, and brought it out under the title of *Octavia*; shortly afterwards he did the same with *Almira*, which was performed in August of the same year. Although Keiser's operas were no more successful than Handel's, and his extravagance and mismanagement forced him to leave Hamburg for three years in order to avoid imprisonment, it is evident that he had made Handel's position in the theatre impossible. Handel withdrew into private life and devoted himself to earning a living by teaching. Mattheson says that Handel remained in Hamburg until 1709, and that he still worked in the theatre, but the first of these statements is certainly untrue, and the second probably so. Mattheson himself left the theatre after the failure of Handel's *Nero*, and his friendship with Handel seems to have come to an end. About Handel's subsequent life in Hamburg we know nothing, until the theatre was taken over by one Saurbrey in the autumn of 1706. Saurbrey commissioned an opera from Handel, but, owing to the confusion in which Keiser had left the affairs of the theatre, it could not be brought out until January 1708, when it was found to be so long that it had to be divided into two operas, *Florindo* and *Daphne*, both of which were put on the stage successively. By that time Handel had left Hamburg for Italy; he evidently took little interest in the production of these works, neither of which has survived.

It was during the run of *Almira*, says Mainwaring, that Handel made the acquaintance of Prince Gian Gastone de' Medici, son of the Grand Duke Cosmo III of Tuscany. Mainwaring's date is wrong, for it is known that Gian Gastone at that time was in Bohemia with his wife, a German princess, to whom he had been married against his will. But it is also known that he was in Hamburg for a few months during the winter of 1703-04, and, if he met Handel at that time, the rest of Mainwaring's story becomes much more credible than subsequent biographers have been willing to admit. According to Mainwaring, Handel became almost an intimate friend of the Prince; they often discussed music together, and the Prince lamented that Handel was unacquainted with the music and musical life of Italy. "Handel confessed that he could see nothing in Italian music which answered the high character His Highness had given it. On the contrary, he thought it so very indifferent, that the singers, he said, must be angels to recommend it." Gian Gastone urged him to come to Italy and hear for himself, intimating "that if he chose to return with him, no conveniences should be wanting." Handel declined the invitation, but resolved to go to Italy as soon as he could do so "on his own bottom."

Gian Gastone was a spendthrift and a profligate; his moral reputation was of the worst, and he was chronically in debt. That, however, would not make it unthinkable that after a glass of wine he should invite Handel to come to Italy with him, but Handel may well have known enough about the Prince even then to reply to the proposal with tactful evasiveness. From what Mattheson says of Handel on his first arrival in Hamburg, it is quite likely that he was contemptuous of Italian opera music, and it is equally likely that after the success of *Almira* his views on Italian opera underwent a change. It is obvious that Hamburg had no further chances to offer him, and the attraction of Italy was at that time so vivid to all young German musicians that not one of them would have refused an opportunity of making the journey.

The date of Handel's departure from Hamburg is unknown, nor have we the slightest information as to his whereabouts until we hear of him at Rome in January 1707. Chrysander's statement that he spent Christmas 1706 with his mother at Halle is manifestly untrue. Mattheson says that he travelled to Rome with a Herr von Binitz, but nothing is known of this gentleman. His most natural route into Italy would be by the Brenner, the historic road of all German pilgrims.

Handel may well have been glad to leave Hamburg, but Hamburg did not forget him. He is mentioned in a theatrical manifesto of 1708 as being already "beloved and celebrated in Italy"; Barthold Feind, one of the Hamburg librettists, who in 1715 translated Handel's *Rinaldo*, called him "the incomparable Handel, the Orpheus of our time"; and from 1715 to 1734 almost all of Handel's London operas were represented on the Hamburg stage.

CHAPTER II

Handel spent three years in Italy. The known facts about his life there are singularly few, and his biographers have often had to draw copiously on their imagination. They may perhaps be forgiven for doing so, since they rightly sought to emphasise the fact that these three years were the most formative period of Handel's personality as a composer. Handel came to Italy as a German; he left Italy an Italian, as far as his music was concerned, and, despite all other influences, Italian was the foundation of his musical language until the end of his life.

On January 14, 1707, a Roman chronicler noted the arrival of "a Saxon, an excellent player on the harpsichord and a composer of music, who has to-day displayed his ability in playing the organ in the church of St. John [Lateran] to the amazement of everyone." This can hardly refer to anyone else than Handel, who throughout his sojourn in Italy was always known as "the Saxon" (*il Sassone*). We owe the discovery of this important document to Mr. Newman Flower. The next date known to us is that of April 11—on the manuscript of Handel's *Dixit Dominus*, composed in Rome.

Most biographers have, however, assumed that Handel's first halt in Italy would have been made at Florence, in view of the fact that Gian Gastone de' Medici is known to have been at Florence from June 1705 to November 1706. The eldest son of the Grand Duke, Prince Ferdinand, was an enthusiastic patron of music, who employed the best musicians of the day to perform operas in his magnificent country palace at Pratolino, some twelve miles north of Florence. It has been suggested that Handel's first Italian opera, *Rodrigo*, was composed for Ferdinand and performed early in 1707, but, in view of Mr. Flower's discovery, this seems unlikely. Mr. Flower suggests, indeed, that Ferdinand did not take much interest in Handel, otherwise he would not have allowed him to go to Rome so soon. This is not impossible, for we know that Ferdinand found the operas of Alessandro Scarlatti too serious for his taste, and he may well have thought even less of Handel's music, which (as we can see from the score of *Rodrigo*) was still very German in style.

Rome could offer Handel no opportunities either for composing operas or even for hearing them. Pope Clement X had permitted the opening of a public opera-house (the Teatro Tordinona) in 1671, but it was closed five years later by Innocent XI, who made every effort he could to suppress opera both in public and in private. Innocent XII, who became Pope in 1691, seems to have been, at first, less intolerant, for the theatre was rebuilt, and a few performances were given; but in 1697 he ordered its destruction on grounds of public morality. Except for a few performances of opera in private in 1701 and 1702 no operas were produced in Rome until 1709.

Deprived of opera, the Romans devoted themselves to oratorio—which in musical style was much the same thing—and to chamber music. The most generous patron of music in Rome was the young Cardinal Ottoboni, who had been raised to the purple in his early twenties, in 1690. He had indeed composed an opera himself, which was performed in 1692, but he was more competent as a poet than as a musician; in 1690 Alessandro Scarlatti had set a libretto of his, *La Statira*.

Handel was no doubt recommended to him by Ferdinand de' Medici, and at the Cardinal's weekly musical parties he soon came into contact with Domenico Scarlatti, as well as with Corelli and Pasquini. Alessandro Scarlatti had left Naples, probably for political reasons, in 1702, and at the end of 1703 Ottoboni had secured him a subordinate post at the church of Santa Maria Maggiore, at the same time appointing him his private director of music. Domenico was a young man of Handel's own age—"a young eagle" as his father called him—brilliantly gifted, and (to judge from Thomas Roseingrave's impression of him) possessed of a singular personal fascination. "Handel," says Mainwaring, "used often to speak of this person with great satisfaction; and indeed there was reason for it; for besides his great talents as an artist, he had the sweetest temper, and the genteelest behaviour." We may indeed regard his friendship with Handel as safely authenticated. It is just possible that Handel may have met Alessandro Scarlatti at Pratolino in the previous autumn, as his opera *Il Gran Tamerlano* was produced there in September; he may well have met him between January and April of 1707. From April to September Alessandro Scarlatti was in Urbino.

Handel's movements now become very difficult to follow. It seems probable that his opera *Rodrigo* was performed at Florence in the autumn of 1707; Mainwaring says that it was composed for Ferdinand de' Medici, but there is no record of any performance at Pratolino. As Handel is said to have been presented to Prince Ernest Augustus of Hanover at Venice, he must have been there in October or November, as the Prince is known to have spent only those two months in that city. Whether Handel remained at Venice over Christmas, or whether he returned to Rome, is uncertain. Domenico Scarlatti is said to have identified him at Venice at a masquerade by his playing of the harpsichord. It would be most natural to suppose then that Handel and the two Scarlattis were in Venice together for the production of Alessandro's two operas, *Mitridate Eupatore* and *Il Trionfo della Libertà*, both of which were brought out at Venice in 1707, but, as it is not known whether this took place at the beginning or at the end of the year, there is not sufficient evidence to support such a conjecture.

During March and April 1708, Handel was the guest of Prince Ruspoli in Rome; this has been definitely ascertained by Mr. Flower. Prince Ruspoli was another great Roman patron of music, and Scarlatti frequently composed works for him; his *Annunciation Oratorio* was performed under his auspices on March 25. On Easter Sunday, April 8, Handel made a triumphal appearance with *La Resurrezione*, which was given on a sumptuous scale, at Ruspoli's expense, in the Palazzo Bonelli, which he was occupying at the time. Corelli led the orchestra.

After *La Resurrezione*, Handel seems to have returned to the patronage of Cardinal Ottoboni, in whose palace he produced a *serenata* (i.e. an allegorical cantata) called *Il Trionfa del Tempo e del Disinganno*, which he remodelled fifty years afterwards as *The Triumph of Time and Truth*. The libretto was by Cardinal Pamphilij. It was the overture to this work which caused so much difficulty to Corelli. Handel, irritated at his lack of understanding, snatched the violin from his hand and played the passage himself, to show how it should be executed; Corelli, gentlest of souls, took no offence, although thirty-two years his senior and the greatest violinist living, but merely observed, "My dear Saxon, this music is in the French style, of which I have no knowledge."

It has been assumed by many biographers that Handel attended the meetings of the Arcadian Academy, and since Prince Ruspoli was a great, benefactor to the Academy, this is extremely probable, although there is no evidence for it. Handel was not a member of the Academy, and various reasons for this have been suggested, such as that he was a foreigner and also too young to be admitted. It is more probable that his admission to that exclusive society was never even contemplated; musicians were generally engaged professionally for the concerts of the Italian academies, but very seldom admitted to the honour of membership. Corelli, Pasquini and Alessandro Scarlatti were all admitted together in 1705; they were the three senior and most distinguished composers of the time, and as no other musicians were then members, it may be assumed that these elections constituted an exceptional honour.

Mainwaring relates that Cardinal Pamphili; on one occasion wrote a poem in honour of Handel and desired him to set it to music himself; in this poem "he was compared to Orpheus, and exalted above the rank of mortals." Later biographers, being unable to trace any music of Handel to this poem, assumed that Handel was too modest to sing his own praises; but he was not, for the original manuscript of the cantata was found by the present writer in the University Library at Münster in Westphalia. As Mainwaring informs us, Handel is compared by the poet (whose name is not given) to Orpheus and indeed exalted above him. "Orpheus," says the Cardinal, "could move rocks and trees, but he could not make them sing; therefore thou art greater than Orpheus, for thou compellest my aged Muse to song." The style of both words and music suggests that the whole cantata was thrown off, as Mainwaring suggests, on the spur of the moment, and this improvisation may well have taken place at one of the Arcadians' garden parties, for there is a well-known account of a similar improvisation by the poet Zappi and the composer Alessandro Scarlatti.

Handel was by this time fully accepted as one of the leading musicians in Italy, for in June he composed a pastoral, *Aci, Galatea e Polifemo*, for the marriage of the Duke of Alvito at Naples on July 19. It was in July 1708 that the Austrian Viceroy of Naples, Count Daun, was succeeded by Cardinal Grimani, who, towards the end of the year, persuaded Alessandro Scarlatti to return to the service of the royal chapel. As a good friend to Scarlatti, the Cardinal was sure to interest himself in Handel, and it was probably through him that Handel was commissioned to write an opera for Venice, as the Grimani were a great Venetian family and owned the principal opera-house there. How long Handel stayed at Naples we do not know; all that Mainwaring tells us is that he was taken up by a Spanish princess, but, as Naples had belonged to Spain for a hundred and fifty years, Spanish princesses can have been no rarities there, and it is impossible to identify this lady.

From July 1708 until December 1709 we lose sight of Handel entirely. On December 26, the first night of the carnival season, his opera *Agrippina* was produced at Venice. The libretto was by Cardinal Grimani, who had already written other dramas for music, all produced, like Handel's, at the Teatro San Giovanni Crisostomo in Venice. Venice was the first city which had undertaken opera on a commercial basis, open to the public on payment, whereas in other places it depended for many years on the munificence of princes and nobles. At Venice there existed not one theatre, but several, devoted to opera, each called after the name of the parish in which it was situated, and, of these, the theatre of St. John Chrysostom, built by the Grimani family and still standing (though much remodelled) under the name of Teatro Malibran, was the largest and most important. The Inquisition took a more tolerant view of opera than the Pope; a Venetian preacher admonished actors and singers to remember that they "were abominated of God, but tolerated by the Government by desire of those who took delight in their iniquities."

Agrippina aroused an extraordinary enthusiasm. "The theatre, at almost every pause, resounded with shouts and acclamations of *viva il taro Sassone!* and other expressions of approbation too extravagant to be mentioned" (Mainwaring). The title part was sung by Margherita Durastanti, and another singer who appeared in the opera was Boschi, the famous bass; both of them were to sing for Handel in London later on. It is fairly certain that Boschi must have sung the part of Polyphemus in Handel's Italian *Aci e Galatea* at Naples, for it bears a striking resemblance to other songs written for Boschi, whose voice was of exceptional range. The opera ran for twenty-seven nights.

After this unprecedented triumph it seems surprising that Handel did not remain in Italy, where he had so many friends who could ensure his success. It is probable that by the time *Agrippina* was performed, if not indeed long before, he had been promised the post of Kapellmeister to the court of Hanover. The actual appointment is dated June 16, 1710. But no sooner was Handel appointed than he at once obtained leave of absence, and went on, first to Düsseldorf, and then to London. It was probably the Elector's intention that he should spend some time in foreign travel before taking up regular duty.

The three years which Handel spent in Italy at the most impressionable period of his life fixed the characteristics of his style as a composer, and we may well suppose that they exercised a decisive influence on his personality and character. His youth had been spent in the respectable middle-class environment of his home at Halle; then came the three years at Hamburg, fantastic and exciting, yet, despite all the artistic stimulus of Keiser's opera-house, inevitably sordid and provincial. Italy introduced him to an entirely different atmosphere—to a life of dignity and serenity in which a classical culture, both literary and artistic, was the matured fruit of wealth, leisure, and good breeding. That exquisite life found its highest musical expression in Alessandro Scarlatti, who at that period was incontestably the greatest of living musicians. On his style Handel formed his own, and it is interesting to note that of all Scarlatti's operas the one which most strikingly foreshadows the genius of Handel is *Mitridate*, which Handel may possibly have seen at Venice in the winter of 1707-08. The musical library of Handel's English friend Charles Jennens contained a large collection of Scarlatti's manuscripts, and there can be little doubt that it was Handel who brought them with him from Italy.

In Venice, Handel had made the acquaintance of Prince Ernest of Hanover, younger brother of the Elector Georg Ludwig who was eventually to become King of England as George I. With Prince Ernest was Baron Kielmansegge, who for many years afterwards remained a firm supporter of Handel, and another Venetian acquaintance was the Duke of Manchester, English Ambassador to the Republic of Venice. Through Prince Ernest, and Kielmansegge, Handel was recommended to the court of Hanover; the Duke of Manchester gave him a pressing invitation to England. Music in Hanover was under the direction of an Italian, Agostino Steffani, who was not only a musician but priest and diplomatist as well. Born at Castelfranco in 1654, he was taken as a boy to Munich, where he studied music, and, in 1680 entered the priesthood; he produced several operas there, and about 1689 became Kapellmeister to the court of Hanover. Here he was employed on important diplomatic business; Pope Innocent XI made him titular Bishop of Spiga in the West Indies, and in 1698 he was Ambassador at Brussels. In 1709 he became the Pope's representative for North Germany, and it was doubtless owing to his heavy ecclesiastical duties that he resigned his musical post in favour of Handel, although Hanover remained his chief place of residence until his death in 1728. He was in Rome in 1708 and 1709, and it has been suggested that he made Handel's acquaintance there, but this hardly seems consistent with Handel's own statement, recorded by Hawkins in his *History of Music*: "When I first arrived at Hanover I was a young man under twenty; I was acquainted with the merits of Steffani and he had heard of me. I understood somewhat of music, and could play pretty well on the organ; he received me with great kindness, and took an early opportunity to introduce me to the Princess Sophia and the Elector's son, giving them to understand that I was what he was pleased to call a virtuoso in music; he obliged me with instructions for my conduct and behaviour during my residence at Hanover; and being called from the city to attend to matters of a public concern, he left me in possession of that favour and patronage which himself had enjoyed for a series of years." These statements of Handel seem, in fact, to point to his having visited Hanover before he went to Italy, possibly before he went to Hamburg, or, more probably, during the course of his Hamburg period, in which case one might conclude that the Electress Sophia had defrayed the cost of Handel's Italian journey. Even if Handel made a mistake as to his age, he clearly implies that his first meeting with Steffani took place in Hanover.

At Düsseldorf, Handel was sure of a warm welcome, for the Elector Johann Wilhelm was a close friend of Steffani, and his wife was a sister of Ferdinand and Gian Gastone de' Medici; he was a man of extravagant tastes, and his opera-house was maintained on the most magnificent scale.

But Handel did not stay there long; England was a greater attraction, and he arrived in London for the first time in the autumn of 1710.

Nothing is known of Handel's early days in London, but it may be safely assumed that he was provided with letters of introduction to persons of influence. We meet him first in the company of Heidegger, a Swiss adventurer who achieved notoriety through his incredible ugliness, and from 1709 onwards was concerned in the management of the opera at the Queen's Theatre in the Haymarket. Through Heidegger, Handel was introduced to Mary Granville, then a little girl of ten, whom he delighted by his performance on her own spinet. Her uncle, Sir John Stanley, asked her if she thought she should ever play as well as Mr. Handel. "If I did not think I should," she cried, "I would burn my instrument!" Mary Granville, who, seven years later, married a Mr. Pendarves, and in 1743 became the wife of Dr. Delany, was for many years one of Handel's most faithful friends and supporters.

In the reign of Queen Anne the musical life of London was developing in a new fashion as compared with what it was in the last twenty years of the previous century. The type of English opera which Purcell and Dryden had created came to an end with Purcell's death in 1695. Italian music, especially when sung by Italian singers, was gradually becoming more and more popular with London concert-audiences, and in 1705 Thomas Clayton produced at Drury Lane an opera called *Arsinoe, Queen of Cyprus*. Clayton had visited Italy, and had brought back with him a collection of Italian songs; he got Peter Motteux to translate for him an old Italian opera libretto, and adapted these songs to it. How much of *Arsinoe* was Clayton's own work is not known; Burney speaks of the opera with nothing but contempt. Yet it seems to have had some fair success, and was even revived the following year; but Clayton's *Rosamond*, to a libretto by Addison, did not survive three performances. It was followed by a series of Italian operas composed by Buononcini, Scarlatti, and others; at first the operas were in English, and sung by English singers, but gradually Italian was introduced, as at Hamburg, and in 1710 an opera called *Almahide*, the music of which Burney ascribes conjecturally to Buononcini, was given in Italian with an entirely Italian company. The victory of the Italians was due mainly to the marvellous singing and acting of Nicola Grimaldi, known as Nicolini, who first appeared in London in Scarlatti's *Pyrrhus and Demetrius*. Nicolini was not the first *castrato* who had been heard in England; the famous Siface had been brought over by Queen Mary of Modena in 1687. But Nicolini was the first who appeared on the English stage, and it was he who paved the way for Senesino, Farinelli, and the rest, and established that annual season of Italian opera which is not yet extinct.

At the time when Handel arrived in London the opera company had migrated from Drury Lane to Vanbrugh's new theatre in the Haymarket, where it was under the management of Aaron Hill, an enterprising young man of Handel's own age who was ready to pursue any sort of career that chance might offer him, whether in literature, music, or business adventure. We may safely hazard a guess that it was Boschi who persuaded Hill to invite Handel to compose an opera for the Queen's Theatre, as Boschi had already sung, in November 1710, in *Hydaspes*, an opera by Francesco Mancini, in which Nicolini delighted his audience in a fight with a lion. Hill sketched a plot based on Tasso's *Jerusalem Delivered*, and an Italian libretto was hastily provided by Giacomo Rossi, Handel composing the music at the same time, and often overtaking the poet. The music, in fact, was completed in a fortnight, and the opera of *Rinaldo* was first produced on the stage on February 24, 1711. To judge from Burney's account of the preceding weeks of the season, coupled with this astonishingly rapid collaboration, it is probable that Hill was in a difficult situation, from which only a new and strikingly successful opera could save him. *Rinaldo* achieved the desired success; it did more, it established Handel's reputation in England as a dramatic composer, and set London a new standard in Italian opera. The previous Italian operas had been works of little distinction, and some of them had even been *pasticcio* operas, as they were called, put together from songs by various composers. Even Scarlatti's *Pyrrhus and Demetrius* paled beside the new opera of Handel, for it had been written as far back as 1694, and was in a style which Scarlatti himself had long abandoned.

Rinaldo had fifteen performances in the course of the season. It provoked bitter attacks from Addison in the *Spectator* and from Steele in the *Tatler*, but everybody knew that Addison's vanity was wounded by the grotesque failure of *Rosamond*, and that Steele had interests in the playhouse. It was useless at that particular moment to champion the cause of English opera, for England happened to possess not a single composer who was equal to the task of writing one.

The opera season came to an end in June, and Handel left London for Germany. He did not go straight back to Hanover, but stayed at Düsseldorf again, where the Elector was evidently desirous of keeping him as long as possible, for the Elector himself wrote more than once to Hanover to make excuses for Handel's prolonged absence from his official duties. Handel may well have felt that Hanover was a dull place as compared with London. There was no opera, and his chief function was to compose Italian chamber duets for the Princess Caroline of Ansbach; afterwards Queen of England. But he may well have taken pleasure in her service, for she was an excellent musician and no mean singer. In November 1711 Handel paid a visit to

Halle, in order to stand godfather to his niece, Johanna Friderica Michaelsen, the daughter of his surviving sister, who eventually inherited the bulk of his fortune. Some biographers have stated that Handel had already revisited his birthplace in 1710 before going to London. Mainwaring is their authority for this, but Mainwaring habitually confused dates and more probably referred to the visit of 1711, for which we have the certain evidence of Friderica Michaelsen's baptismal register. It is clear that the alleged visit of 1710 was suggested merely by a desire to make the most of Handel's affection for his mother, which Mainwaring had already emphasised. Mainwaring, however, went beyond the truth in saying that she had become blind; she did eventually lose her sight, but not until some twenty years later.

Handel appears to have remained at Hanover until the autumn of 1712, when he obtained permission to go to London again "on condition that he engaged to return within a reasonable time" (Mainwaring). What period was to be considered reasonable we do not know. Handel had certainly been planning this London visit for some time, as he was corresponding with friends in England, and was also taking some trouble to improve his knowledge of the English language. It is not surprising that he hankered after London, for London offered him a society which bore more resemblance to the world which he had known at Rome. The tradition of Italian culture had for generations been more firmly implanted in England than anywhere in Germany, except perhaps in Vienna, and, since those three years in Italy, Handel's musical outlook had become completely Italian, as his music shows. The few attempts which he made at German Church music present a curious contrast of style; one could hardly believe them to be the work of that Handel whom we have adopted as our own. German music at that date was provincial; Italian music was the music of the great world, because it was the music of the theatre. It was to the theatre that Handel looked forward, and London had what even Rome had not—an opera, and an Italian opera. The success of *Rinaldo* had shown him that London was the place where he might launch out into a triumphal career as a composer for the stage.

CHAPTER III

For the greater part of the nineteenth century the Handelian type of opera was the laughingstock of musical critics; they wondered how any audiences could have endured to sit through it, and why the fashionable society of London should have neglected native music for what Dr. Johnson defined as "an exotic and irrational entertainment." The modern reader's impression of an Italian opera of Handel's days is a story about some ancient or mediaeval hero whose very name is often to most people unknown; if he happens to be someone as famous as Julius Caesar, the familiar episodes of his life are sacrificed to some imaginary and complicated intrigue presented in the form of long and elaborate songs, thinly accompanied, and separated by stretches of dreary recitative. But in those days persons of culture, in England as well as in Italy, were perhaps more interested in ancient history and in the history of the later Roman Empire than they are now; it is significant that Gibbon's *Decline and Fall* made its appearance just when the fashion for operas on subjects which might have been taken from its pages was coming to an end.

The conventional treatment of those subjects, which makes all the operas seem exactly alike, was the result of a certain literary reform which had tended to standardise opera libretti under the influence of Racine, and it was really a movement towards dignity and dramatic unity after the monstrous confusion of the earlier Venetian operas. As to the conventionality of the music, and its forms of air and recitative, it can only be said that all serious Italian music was written in these forms; it was simply the normal musical style of the period, and must have been as natural to its own audiences as the style of Puccini or Richard Strauss at the present day. Handelian opera has often been described as a concert in costume, and Dr. Burney, writing as late as 1789, both admits this description and defends it.

"An opera, at the worst, is still better than a concert merely for the ear, or a pantomime entertainment for the eye. Supposing the articulation to be wholly unintelligible, we have an excellent union of melody and harmony, vocal as well as instrumental, for the ear. And, according to Sir Richard Steele's account of Nicolini's action, 'it was so significant, that a deaf man might go along with him in the sense of the part he acted.'

"No one will dispute but that understanding Italian would render our entertainment at an opera more rational and more complete; but without that advantage, let it be remembered by the lovers of Music, that an opera is the *completest concert* to which they can go; with this advantage over those in still life, that to the most perfect singing, and effects of a powerful and well-disciplined band, are frequently added excellent acting, splendid scenes and decorations, with such dancing as a playhouse, from its inferior prices, is seldom able to furnish."

Orchestral concerts in those days did not exist; concerts of any kind were rare, and the best were to be heard in that historic room over Thomas Britton's small coal shop, in Clerkenwell, where Handel himself sometimes played on a chamber-organ for the genuine musical enthusiasts of London society. It was no wonder that Italian opera became fashionable. Italian singers have always been unrivalled in popular favour, and in Handel's days they were not only something new to England, but were the exponents of a vocal art which admittedly has never been surpassed. The theatre was new and sumptuous; society was wealthy and at the same time exclusive; at the opera the great world met together as in a sort of club. People went to talk and to be seen as well as to see and hear; they do so in certain opera-houses still. And the Queen's Theatre in the Haymarket possessed the greatest opera-composer living, a greater even than Scarlatti himself.

It was a period when there was still a considerable tradition of musicianship among the amateurs of English society. Old Countess Granville, known to her younger relatives as "the Dragon," who had lived all through the age of Locke and Purcell, wrote, at the age of eighty, to her cousin Mrs. Pendarves—Handel's child friend Mary Granville—in 1734: "There is, I think, no accomplishment so great for a lady as music, for it tunes the mind." There were plenty of people in the great houses capable of appreciating the merits of Handel, or at any rate of constituting themselves his enemies.

Handel must have arrived in England at least as early as the beginning of October 1712, for the manuscript of *Il Pastor Fido*, the first new opera which he produced, is dated, at the end, "Londres, ce 24 Octobre." The opera-house was now under the management of Owen MacSwiney, who seems to have been both incompetent and unreliable. *Il Pastor Fido* did not attract the public, and was withdrawn after six performances, but Handel soon had another opera ready to take its place. *Teseo* was finished on December 19, and brought out on January 10, 1713; it was a romantic-heroic opera, closely modelled on *Rinaldo*, with an abundance of scenic effects. After the second performance MacSwiney disappeared, leaving the singers unpaid as well as the scene-painters and costume-makers. The company carried on the season undeterred, and the management was taken over by Heidegger. Handel's opera was performed twelve times—on the last night for the composer's benefit; between the acts he gave a performance himself on the harpsichord.

For the moment, however, the operatic situation was not encouraging, and Handel turned his thoughts in other directions. He had stayed first at the London house of a Mr. Andrews of Barn Elms in Surrey, but he soon transferred himself to the house of Lord Burlington in Piccadilly. Lord Burlington was only seventeen years of age, but he and his mother made Burlington House an artistic and literary centre comparable with the palaces of Cardinal Ottoboni and Prince Ruspoli at Rome. As the libretto of *Teseo* is dedicated to him, he must have taken Handel under his patronage soon after his arrival in England, but the precise date at which Handel went to live with him is uncertain. According to Hawkins, he stayed at Burlington House for three years, meeting Pope, Gay, and Dr. Arbuthnot, as well as many other "men of the first eminence for genius." But Gay does not seem to have met Lord Burlington until 1715, and Pope mentions him first in 1718. It is thought that Handel's little opera, *Silla*, may have been written for a private performance at Burlington House in 1714, and the dedication of *Amadigi*, Handel's next opera (1715), indicates that the music was composed within his patron's own walls.

One of Handel's favourite haunts in London was St. Paul's Cathedral, where Brind the organist often persuaded him to play the organ after evening service, to the great delight of the congregation. He appears to have made Brind's acquaintance first through young Maurice Greene, then aged seventeen, who had been a chorister of St. Paul's, and, after his voice broke in 1710, was articled to Brind as a pupil. After service was over, Handel, Greene, and some of the members of the choir would repair to the Queen's Arms Tavern close by for an evening of music and musical conversation.

This friendly association with St. Paul's was no doubt of great value to Handel in his next musical undertakings—the *Birthday Ode* for Queen Anne, and the *Te Deum* which celebrated the Peace of Utrecht in 1713. The Queen's patronage may very likely have been obtained for him by Lady Burlington, as she was one of the Ladies of the Bedchamber. These two works are important landmarks in Handel's career, as they were his first compositions to English words, and his first compositions for English ceremonial occasions. They marked him out as the natural successor to Purcell, and it is evident that in each case he took Purcell's similar composition as his model. Up till now he had been a foreigner engaged to provide Italian opera for the amusement of fashionable society; with the *Birthday Ode* he became a court musician to the Queen of England, and with the *Te Deum* his music entered St. Paul's.

The practical result of the *Ode* was a pension of £200 a year conferred on him by Queen Anne. It is clear that he now regarded England as his permanent home, regardless of the fact that he was officially the servant of the Elector of Hanover and had undertaken to return thither "within a reasonable time." But on August 1, 1714, the Queen died, and the Elector was proclaimed King of England. When George I came over to his new country, Handel did not dare to show himself at court, and all efforts on the part of his friends to effect a reconciliation with the King were in vain. The King went to see his new opera, *Amadigi*, which came out late in the season of 1715, but refused to pardon him, until Handel's old Venetian acquaintance, Baron Kielmansegge, now Master of the Horse, devised an ingenious expedient for surprising the King into clemency.

One of the favourite amusements of London society was to make up a water-party on the Thames, with a band of musicians in attendance. Mrs. Pendarves describes a party of this kind in July 1722; they rowed up to Richmond, where they had supper, and "were entertained all the time by very good music [for wind instruments] in another barge." Baron Kielmansegge arranged that the King should go for an excursion of this kind, and that, without his knowledge, Handel should conduct appropriate music of his own in a barge that followed the King's. As the Baron was often in charge of the music for such occasions, this can have been a matter of no great difficulty; in any case it achieved the desired result. The King was enchanted with the music, and restored Handel to favour. As Mainwaring tells this story just before speaking of *Amadigi*, it has generally been assumed that this episode took place in the summer of 1715, but more recently it has been ascribed to 1717, on the strength of a long account of a royal water-party, with music by Handel, given in the *Daily Courant*, a newspaper of the period. This account was copied by the Envoy of Brandenburg at the court of St. James's and despatched by him to Berlin; the discovery of this document has led certain writers to cast doubt on Mainwaring's story. Streatfeild is probably right in suggesting that Mainwaring's story refers to an earlier water-party, and that Handel contributed music frequently for such occasions. He also points out that the celebrated *Water Music* was not published until 1740, and that it may quite well have been collected from various aquatic programmes.

Hawkins relates the story of the *Water Music*, evidently copying from Mainwaring; but Hawkins had known Handel personally, and had been supplied by him with certain reminiscences, one of which was unknown to Mainwaring. According to this anecdote, recorded by Hawkins, the reconciliation with George I was due to the violinist Geminiani, who had composed a set of sonatas dedicated to Baron Kielmansegge; Geminiani was a notoriously difficult player to accompany, and insisted on Handel, and no other, taking the harpsichord when he went to play the sonatas to the King.

Mr. Flower, in his life of Handel, refuses all credit to Mainwaring's well-known tale, and takes the view that the King never had any quarrel with Handel at all. In any case it seems certain that he confirmed the pension granted to him by Queen Anne, and added a further £200 a year of his own. A few years later, Handel received yet another £200 a year—from Caroline of Ansbach, now Princess of Wales, for teaching her daughters the harpsichord, so that he enjoyed a settled income of £600 a year for the rest of his life.

Amadigi, produced May 25, 1715, did not have many performances, as the season ended on July 9, but it attracted considerable attention, partly because that old favourite, Nicolini, sang in it again, and also on account of its elaborate staging. "There is more enchantment and machinery in this opera," says Dr. Burney, "than I have ever found to be announced in any other musical drama performed in England."

During the following season, which did not begin until February 1716, both *Rinaldo* and *Amadigi* were revived, but Handel produced no new opera. The King seems to have wished to see Nicolini in his older parts; *Pyrrhus and Demetrius* was revived, as well as other operas of the days before Handel's first arrival in England. In July, at the end of the season, George I returned to Hanover, where he remained until the end of the year. Handel accompanied him, but seems to have had freedom to travel, for he visited Hamburg, where he avoided meeting his old friend Mattheson, though he corresponded with him from a safe distance. He also went to Halle, where his mother was still living; Zachow, however, was dead, and had left his widow in straitened circumstances, with an idle and intemperate son. Handel helped the widow, and continued to send her money in later years, but he eventually came to the conclusion that it was useless to do anything for the son. From Halle he went on to Ansbach, no doubt on some commission from the Princess of Wales. At Ansbach he found an old friend from the University of Halle, Johann Christoph Schmidt, who was established in a woollen business. Although Schmidt was married and had a family, he was persuaded by Handel to leave these behind at Ansbach and to travel with him to London, where he spent the rest of his life as Handel's faithful secretary and copyist. His son came over later on, and, after Handel had provided for his education, assisted his father in looking after Handel during his old age.

During these six months in Germany, Handel reverted for a moment to German music; he set what is known as the *Brockes Passion*, a sacred cantata in verse by the Hamburg poet Brockes, which had already been set once by Keiser. Later on it was set to music again by two of Handel's former friends, first by Telemann, and then by Mattheson. Little is known about the composition of this work; Handel apparently had a copy made after his return to England and sent this to Mattheson, and it was performed at Hamburg in 1717. Handel does not seem to have had it performed in England; he used up the music afterwards for other works. Chrysander attributed to 1716 a set of nine German songs with violin *obbligato* to semi-sacred words by Brockes; but there is some difficulty about accepting this date, for, although eight of the poems had already been printed by Brockes, there is one which is found only in the second edition of the book, printed in 1724.

The King came back to London in January 1717, and it is supposed that Handel came with him. The opera was on the verge of collapse. *Rinaldo* and *Amadigi* were once more revived for Nicolini, but Handel contributed no new work, and, after the season came to an end in July, there was no more Italian opera in London until 1720. It was during this period that Handel became musical director to the Duke of Chandos, for whom he composed works of a character new both to England and to himself.

James Brydges, first Duke of Chandos, had built himself an Italian palace at Canons, near Edgware, in which he must have outdone even the magnificent Lord Burlington in sumptuousness and ostentation. Like a German princeling, he kept his choir and his band of musicians, though there seems to be no evidence that he was himself genuinely musical. The chapel of the house, a florid Italian baroque building with frescoes in the appropriate style by Italian painters, was opened in 1720, and the anthem for the occasion was no doubt one of Handel's. It is not known what music of Handel's was performed at the Duke's private concerts, but for the services of the chapel he composed the famous *Chandos Te Deum* and the twelve *Chandos Anthems*. Here again Purcell was his model, but the style was Handel's own, a style indeed so appropriate to the formal stateliness of the Duke's establishment that these works have never become part of the ordinary cathedral repertory. It was to Purcell, and to some extent to Scarlatti too, that Handel owed the general plan of the anthems with their orchestral accompaniments, but even Purcell's anthems with orchestra had by that time been found too elaborate for general use.

To the Chandos period belongs also a work which is still one of Handel's most popular compositions, the English *Acis and Galatea*, to words by John Gay. It was not a revision of the *serenata* which he wrote at Naples, but an entirely new work. More important as a landmark in Handel's development is the masque of *Esther*, originally called *Haman and Mordecai*. About the early history of these works little is known; both were intended to be acted on the stage, and they were very probably performed in this way at Canons. The words of *Esther* were adapted from Racine's play of the same name, and it has been suggested that Pope was the author.

Handel's residence at Canons gave rise to two legends about him which are still so often repeated that their absurdity must be mentioned here, although they have been known for many years to be baseless. One is perpetuated by an inscription on the organ in the church at Whitchurch, to the effect that Handel composed the oratorio of *Esther* on this instrument. Handel was never organist at Whitchurch; the church existed in his day, but it was an entirely separate building from the private chapel of the Duke of Chandos which was pulled down with the house. The organ of that chapel is now at Gosport. It need hardly be said that in any case it was not Handel's practice to compose his works on an organ. The other, and even more popular, legend is that of "The Harmonious Blacksmith." It was during the Canons period that Handel published his *Suites de Pièces pour le Clavecin* (1720) which had probably been composed for the daughters of the Princess of Wales, and one of these suites contains the air and variations known by that familiar title. But the air was never called by this name before 1820; about that time a young music-seller at Bath, who had previously been a blacksmith's apprentice, earned the nickname of "the harmonious blacksmith" because he was always singing that particular tune. Somehow the name got transferred from the singer to the song, and in 1835 the story of Handel's having been inspired to compose the tune after hearing a blacksmith at Edgware produce musical notes from his anvil was first put into print in a letter to *The Times*. Not long afterwards an imaginary blacksmith of Edgware was invented, and his alleged anvil sold by auction.

Whether the air is Handel's own composition at all is a matter of uncertainty; there would be nothing in the least unusual about any composer taking another man's air as a theme for variations, and it has been suggested, with some plausibility, that the tune is that of an old French song.

On August 8, 1718, Handel's sister Dorothea Sophia died of consumption at Halle. She was not more than thirty years of age; the other sister, Johanna, had died in 1709. The sermon preached at Dorothea's funeral on August 11, 1718, has been preserved, and tells us that one of her favourite texts from the Bible, which she was often in the habit of quoting, was, "I know that my Redeemer liveth." Chrysander suggested, and we may well believe, that the setting of these words in *Messiah*, given to a female voice, owed its inspiration to the memory of Dorothea Sophia. Handel was evidently much attached to her. To attend her funeral was impossible, and it was some months before Handel could visit Halle again; but on February 20, 1719, he wrote a letter to his brother-in-law, thanking him for all the kindness which he had shown to his sister, and promising to come to Halle as soon as his engagements permitted.

Handel's inability to leave London before February 1719 was due to the fact that a new scheme for the promotion of opera in London was on foot. The first idea was probably suggested in the circle of the Duke of Chandos towards the end of 1718. It was the moment of the South Sea Bubble, and speculation had become the universal fashion. To revive the Italian opera a company was formed among members of the nobility; a capital of £50,000 was raised in shares of £100 each, and the King himself contributed £1,000. The new venture was called the Royal Academy of Music, in imitation of the *Académie Royale de Musique*, under which name the Paris opera was officially known. The French designation was obviously suggested by the Italian "academies," or literary and musical societies of the period; the expression *accademia di musica* is still occasionally used in Italy to signify a concert. The directors engaged Nicolo Haym and Paolo Rolli as poets to provide libretti; for the music they naturally secured Handel, but also invited Buononcini over from Rome, and Attilio Ariosti from Berlin. Handel was sent at once to Dresden to select singers; on February 21 he is stated to have left London for that purpose, but it is possible that he may actually have started later, for in his letter to his brother-in-law, dated February 20, he says, "I beg you will not judge of my desire to see you by the delay of my departure, for to my great regret I find myself detained here by important business on which I may say my fortune depends, and it has dragged on longer than I expected.... I hope I shall be at the end of it in a month from now."

Handel's exact itinerary is difficult to establish. We know that he went to Düsseldorf, where he engaged the singer Baldassari, but whether this was on the outward journey or later in the year is uncertain. From the letter to Michaelsen we should imagine that he went to Halle as soon as possible; the only authentic document which gives us any date is a letter from Count Flemming, a court functionary at Dresden, to Melusine von Schulenburg, daughter of George I's mistress the Duchess of Kendal, who in 1733 married Lord Chesterfield. Melusine was a pupil of Handel in London. The letter is dated from Dresden, October 6, 1719; the Count seems to have been much offended by Handel's behaviour, and suggests that he was "a little mad" (*un peu fol*). Count Flemming was evidently vain of his own musicianship, and this made him feel all the more hurt at Handel's obstinate refusal to accept his invitations. The Electoral Prince of Saxony was married about this time to an Austrian Archduchess, and the Elector had invited several of the most famous Italian singers, headed by the composer Lotti, to Dresden to grace the occasion, hoping to make contracts with them for the winter season.

Handel's object in Dresden was to tempt these celebrities to London by the offer of English guineas, so that he was naturally obliged to be extremely discreet in his relations with the officials of the court.

He certainly played the harpsichord at court, for in the following February (1720) a sum of 100 ducats was paid to him; this however cannot indicate that he was actually in Dresden at that date, and may easily have been a delayed payment for earlier services. Handel's negotiations with the singers were only moderately successful, for he was unable to secure anyone except Signora Durastanti for the opening of the London opera, even though that was delayed until April 1720. The others remained at Dresden, but it is probable that Handel's offers had not been without their attractions, for the Italian singers at Dresden gave so much trouble to the management that the Elector suddenly dismissed the whole crew in February 1720; none of them, however, appeared in London before the autumn season.

Handel's visit to Halle this year is of peculiar interest because of the attempt made by J. S. Bach to become acquainted with him. Forkel's biography of Bach (1802) is the only authority for this story. Bach in 1719 was in the service of the Prince of Anhalt-Cöthen; hearing that Handel was in the neighbourhood, he went over to Halle, a distance of about twenty miles, but found that Handel had already departed for London. The exact date of Handel's return is not known, but as there was a meeting of the shareholders of the opera on November 6, 1719, he may have been in England by that time. He was not himself one of the actual directors of the company; the only professional member of the board was Heidegger. Burney suggests that the affairs of the company were none too prosperous even before the season began; and it is strange that so long a delay took place between the first initiation of the scheme in the winter of 1718 and the first rise of the curtain on April 2, 1720. Handel, at any rate, must have felt his own position to be secure, for it was about this time that he took the house at what was then 57 Lower Brook Street, Grosvenor Square, where he resided for the rest of his life. His name appears first in 1725 among the ratepayers of the parish of St. George's, Hanover Square, but not long ago a lead cistern was found in the house, bearing his initials and the date 1721. On what terms he took the house is not known; it is not mentioned in his will.

CHAPTER IV

The opening performance of the Royal Academy of Music was undistinguished; it is hard to understand why the noble directors should have begun their season with *Numitor*, an opera by Porta, a Venetian composer, who is described in the book of words as "Servant to His Grace the Duke of Wharton." The Duke of Wharton was not one of the directors. The company, moreover, was more English than Italian; it included Baldassari, Durastanti, and a second woman called Galerati, together with Anastasia Robinson, who afterwards became Countess of Peterborough, Mrs. Turner Robinson, wife of the organist of Westminster Abbey, Mrs. Dennis, and Mr. Gordon. *Numitor* ran for five performances; on April 27 it was succeeded by Handel's new opera *Radamisto*, in which the same singers took part, except that Mrs. Dennis did not appear, and Mr. La Garde sang the part of Farasmane. It is interesting to note that two of the male parts were taken by women—Radamisto (Durastanti) and Tigrane (Galerati). This looks as if the management had found it impossible to secure a sufficient number of Italian *castrati*, who probably demanded exorbitant fees.

Radamisto fared little better than *Numitor*; an enormous crowd came to the first night, and many were turned away, but the opera was not performed more than ten times in the season. It was probably above the heads of the audience, for it is one of Handel's finest works for the stage and a great advance on any of his previous operas. The only other opera performed was *Narciso*, by Domenico Scarlatti, which was even less successful than the others. Chrysander seems to suggest that Scarlatti came to London with the idea of being a rival to Handel, but it is much more likely that Handel himself persuaded the Academy to invite the friend of his youth.

The season ended on June 25. *Radamisto* was printed, and was published by Handel himself at his own house.

A really serious rival to Handel appeared in the autumn. Lord Burlington had made the acquaintance in Rome of Giovanni Buononcini, and had heard his opera *Astarto*. Perhaps he had had enough of Handel after three years of his close company in Burlington House; in any case he probably thought himself a better judge of music than Handel. He secured Buononcini for the Academy, and the season opened on November 19 with

Astarto. The dedication to the Earl of Burlington is signed by Paolo Rolli, and no other author's name is mentioned; but the libretto was really by Apostolo Zeno (1708). *Astarto* had ten performances before Christmas, and twenty afterwards; *Radamisto* was revived again, but Buononcini established himself firmly in the favour of a large party. Although Burney speaks very disparagingly of the music, it is not in the least surprising that the opera attracted the public. In the first place, it had the advantage of a magnificent cast of singers—Senesino, Boschi, Berenstadt, Berselli, Durastanti, Salvai, and Galerati, and this sudden blaze of vocal splendour would in itself have made the success of any opera, especially of one which opened the season. Besides, Buononcini's music was pleasing and, after a far longer stage experience than Handel's, he naturally wrote what singers enjoyed singing. It must further be added that Buononcini himself was a striking personality; he had produced operas at Berlin and Vienna, as well as in various Italian cities, and was a man of the world, accustomed to the society of courts. Besides, Buononcini was a stranger and a novelty; Handel was becoming an established institution—indeed, he was well on the way to becoming an English composer.

The same singers, with the addition of Anastasia Robinson, appeared in the season of 1721-22. A curious experiment was tried in *Muzio Scevola*, of which the first act was composed by Filippo Mattei, the second by Buononcini and the third by Handel, each act having an overture and concluding chorus. Some biographers have supposed that this was intended to be a trial of strength, and that the contest resulted in the acknowledged triumph of Handel; but Burney is probably right in saying that the collaboration was merely a device to save time in getting the opera ready, and Burney further points out that Buononcini's position remained as strong as ever. It was in fact due to Buononcinci's next two operas, and not to Handel's, that the Academy was able to declare a dividend of seven per cent.

Handel's *Floridante* (December 9, 1721) had a moderate success only, and against Handel's one opera (except for a few performances of *Radamisto* at the very beginning of the season) Buononcini had three works to his credit. The following season brought Handel better fortune, and a decline in the popularity of Buononcini. In November and December, *Muzio Sceaola* and *Floridante* were revived; on January 12, Handel produced a new opera, *Ottone*, with a new singer, Francesca Cuzzoni, who eclipsed all the other women singers completely, until after some years she herself was driven into eclipse by her historic rival Faustina Bordoni.

Ottone contains one number at least which is familiar to everyone who knows the name of Handel—the gavotte at the end of the overture.

This spirited piece of music won popularity at the outset, and even to-day it is probably the best known melody of Handel, after the "Harmonious Blacksmith." But the real success of *Ottone* was made by Cuzzoni.

How Cuzzoni came to be engaged at the opera is not clear. Handel cannot possibly have ever heard her sing; it has been suggested that she was engaged by Heidegger. She was about twenty-two, and had made her first appearance at Venice in 1719, after which she sang in various Italian theatres. She had a voice of extraordinary range, beauty, and agility; she was equally accomplished both in florid music and in airs of a sustained and pathetic character, and she was never known to sing out of tune. In appearance she was anything but attractive: she was short, squat, and excessively plain-featured. She was uneducated and ill-mannered, impulsive and quarrelsome. Her arrival in London was delayed for some reason, so the management sent Sandoni, the second harpsichord-player, to meet her, probably at Dover. On the way to London they were married; Sandoni doubtless had an eye to the money which she was to earn.

Her first air in *Ottone*, "Falsa imagine," fixed her reputation as an expressive and pathetic singer (Burney); she had at first refused to sing it, on which Handel remarked to her, "Madame, je sais que vous êtes une véritable diablesse, mais je vous ferai savoir, moi, que je suis Béelzebub, le chef des diables," seized her round and waist, and threatened to throw her out of the window. Handel had similar trouble with Gordon, the English singer who came in for a small part in *Flavio*, which was given on May 14. Gordon found fault with Handel's method of accompanying, and threatened to jump on the harpsichord.

"Oh," replied Handel, "let me know when you will do that, and I will advertise it; for I am sure more people will come to see you jump than to hear you sing."

Two more operas by Buononcini were given, but his relations with the Academy were not very cordial. He had been taken up by the Marlborough family, and was commissioned to compose the funeral anthem for the burial of the great Duke in June 1722. On May 16, 1723, Mrs. Pendarves informed her sister that the young Duchess had settled £500 a year for life on Buononcini, "provided he will *not* compose any more for the ungrateful Academy, who do not deserve he should entertain them, since they don't know how to value his works as they ought." The contract, however, seems not to have been carried out by the composer. Mrs. Pendarves evidently took the news from the day's issue of a weekly journal, adding only the name of the Duchess, which the paper had suppressed. What the paper tells us is that the Academy had not engaged Buononcini for the coming season.

Senesino and Cuzzoni had made life impossible for the other singers. Durastanti retired to the Continent; Anastasia Robinson left the stage, and married her old admirer Lord Peterborough. Senesino and Cuzzoni, however, were indispensable to the success of the opera, and probably the ridiculous affectations of the one and the abominable manners of the other were not without their attraction to a public which could enjoy all the pleasure of gossiping about them without having to put up with them at close quarters.

The season of 1723 began in November with Buononcini's *Farnace* and Handel's *Ottone*; in January 1724 a new opera, *Vespasiano*, by Attilio Ariosti, was given, and ran for nine successive nights. Ariosti was never a very troublesome rival to Handel; he was a man of amiable character, and apparently quite content to remain aloof from the party politics of the opera-house. On February 14, Handel produced his *Giulio Cesare*, one of his finest dramatic works; it has been revived with considerable success in recent years, partly owing to the fact that modern audiences are more familiar with the episode of Caesar and Cleopatra than with the subjects of Handel's other operas. *Giulio Cesare* had the advantage of a strong cast; Senesino sang the title part, with Berenstadt and Boschi to support him, and the women included Cuzzoni, as well as Durastanti and Mrs. Robinson, who had not yet quitted the opera company.

Another masterpiece of Handel's, *Tamerlano*, inaugurated the autumn season of 1724 in October; in December appeared Ariosti's *Artaserse*, in January *Giulio Cesare* held the stage till the production of another Handel opera, *Rodelinda*, which came out on February 13, and ran for thirteen nights. Two more operas, by Ariosti and Leonardo Vinci of Naples, completed the season, but it was evidently Handel who scored the greatest triumphs, unless the honours should more properly go to Cuzzoni, as Rodelinda, and her brown silk gown trimmed with silver. All the old ladies, says Burney, were scandalised with its vulgarity and indecorum, "but the young adopted it as a fashion so universally, that it seemed a national uniform for youth and beauty."

Cuzzoni created a further sensation in the summer by giving birth to a daughter. Mrs. Pendarves made much fun of the event. "It is a mighty mortification it was not a son. Sons and heirs ought to be out of fashion when such scrubs shall pretend to be dissatisfied at having a daughter; 'tis pity, indeed, that the noble name and family of the Sandonis should be extinct! The minute she was brought to bed she sang' La speranza,' a song in *Otho*."

Revivals of *Rodelinda* and *Ottone* took place in the following season, and, in March 1726, Handel produced *Scipio*, in which the famous march was heard for the first time on the rise of the curtain.

But Cuzzoni's throne was soon to be sharply contested. Ever since 1723 the directors of the opera had been trying to secure Faustina Bordoni, and at last, with a promise of £2,500 for the season (Cuzzoni received £2,000), they succeeded. Faustina was born of a patrician family at Venice in 1700; she had been brought up under the protection of Alessandro Marcello, brother of the well-known composer, and had made her debut at Venice at the age of sixteen. She sang mostly at Venice for several years, and in 1718 she appeared there in Pollaroli's *Ariodante*, along with Cuzzoni herself. She sang at Munich in 1723, and in the summer of 1725 she went to Vienna, where she stayed six months, enjoying an extraordinary success. Nearly forty years afterwards the Empress Maria Theresa recalled with pride how she herself, at the age of seven, had sung in an opera with Faustina. At the end of March 1726 she left Vienna for London, where she made her first appearance, on May 5, in Handel's new opera *Alessandro*, which had been designed especially to show off both Faustina and Cuzzoni in parts of exactly equal importance and difficulty. The immediate result was to divide London society into two parties: young Lady Burlington and her friends supported Faustina; Cuzzoni's admirers were led by Lady Pembroke. Lady Walpole succeeded in getting both to sing at her house; neither would sing in the presence of the other, but the hostess tactfully managed to draw first one and then the other out of the music-room while her rival enchanted the guests. Mrs. Pendarves also contrived to be on good terms with both. She heard Cuzzoni in November privately, or perhaps at a rehearsal, and writes, "my senses were ravished with harmony." The opera was expected to begin about the middle of December, "but I think Faustina and Madame Sandoni [i.e. Cuzzoni] are not perfectly agreed about their parts." The opening, however, was delayed by the absence of Senesino, who had gone to Italy and did not return until fairly late in December.

It was probably owing to this fact that opera in English was offered at the theatre in Lincoln's Inn Fields, where Marcantonio Buononcini's *Camilla*, first given in London in 1706, was revived by a mainly English cast of singers. Mrs. Pendarves went to see it, and her criticisms are significant for the taste of the time. "I can't say I was much pleased with it, I liked it for old acquaintance sake, but there is not many of the songs better than ballads."

Faustina—"the most agreeable creature in the world in company"— dined with Mrs. Pendarves for a small musical party on January 26. On the previous day there was the first rehearsal of Handel's *Admeto*. It was the moment, says Burney, of Handel's greatest prosperity and English patronage. *Admeto* exhibited conspicuously what Dr. Burney called Handel's "science "; it was evidently considered to be complicated in style, though at the same time both pathetic and passionate. "Music," says Burney, "was no longer regarded as a mere soother of affliction, or incitement to hilarity; it could now paint the passions in all their various attitudes; and those tones which said nothing intelligible to the heart began to be thought as; insipid as those of 'sounding brass or tinkling cymbals.'" These words of Burney make one realise that Handel's London operas must have affected their audiences almost in the way in which the operas of Wagner startled the audiences of the nineteenth century. Handel himself, like Wagner, was steadily developing his own dramatic powers, and it is important to bear in mind that it was only those marvellous singers of Handel's day, such as Senesino, Cuzzoni, Faustina, and Boschi, who could inspire him to the creation of such music as they only were competent to interpret.

Admeto was received with respect, and although the partisans of the "rival queens" were noisy in their applause, no actual disturbance took place until Admeto was followed by Buononcini's *Astyanax* on May 6. On the first night of the new opera each side did its best to drown the opposite party's favourite with a chorus of catcalls. The behaviour of the audience became more and more disgraceful as the opera was repeated, until on the last night (June 6), when the Princess of Wales was present, Cuzzoni and Faustina delighted the sporting instincts of the nobility and gentry of England by indulging in a free fight on the stage.

Five days later George I died suddenly at Osnabruck. George II was crowned on October 11, to the music of Handel's Coronation Anthems. The opera season reopened a month later. Apparently the quarrel between Cuzzoni and Faustina had been patched up; probably neither of them wanted to lose their English contracts. They appeared together in Handel's *Riccardo Primo*, and again in *Siroe* (February 5, 1728), as well as in *Tolomeo* (April 30), but the battle seems to have been won by Cuzzoni, who obtained the more important parts. We hear of no more disturbances; the fact was that the audiences were too thin to be noisy.

Mrs. Pendarves, always a devoted supporter of Handel, was pessimistic from the beginning of the season. "I doubt operas will not survive longer than this winter," she wrote on November 25; "they are now at their last gasp; the subscription is expired and nobody will renew it. The directors are always squabbling, and they have so many divisions among themselves that I wonder they have not broke up before; Senesino goes away next winter, and I believe Faustina, so you see harmony is almost out of fashion." *Admeto* was revived on June 1, 1728; this was Faustina's last appearance, and the last night of the Royal Academy of Music. The opera was announced for June 11, but Faustina declared herself indisposed. The opera was shut up and the company disbanded. Faustina went with Senesino to Paris, and thence to Venice, where Cuzzoni also made her appearance, and continued in the local dialect the campaign of slander against Faustina's alleged immoralities.

There were many reasons for the collapse of the opera. It had been carried on with reckless extravagance, and the noble directors were in all probability not very expert men of business. The scandalous behaviour of all concerned in *Astyanax* may well have caused a falling-off in the subscriptions. Mrs. Pendarves, who was a lady of unimpeachable conduct, continued to go to the opera, but she was a serious lover of music and a personal friend of Handel. The failure of the Academy is generally attributed to the success of *The Beggar's Opera*, which had been brought out at Lincoln's Inn Fields on January 29, 1728, and at once took London by storm. A letter of Mrs. Pendarves, dated January 19, but evidently continued later, tells us that she went to a rehearsal of *Siroe*: "I like it extremely, but the taste of the town is so depraved, that nothing will be approved of but the burlesque. The *Beggar's Opera* entirely triumphs over the Italian one." Even Mrs. Pendarves could not help enjoying it, once she had seen it.

It is probable that Handel himself had contributed to the downfall of the Academy. Out of the 487 performances given between 1720 and 1728, Handel's works obtained 245, Buononcini's 108, and Ariosti's 55. The great singers had drawn the public to listen to Handel's operas, but it is clear from many contemporary allusions that Handel's music was too severe to be an attraction in itself, except to cultivated musicians like Mrs. Pendarves. The same accusations were made against Handel that were made in later years against Mozart and Wagner—that his operas were noisy and overloaded with learned accompaniments. The Italian opera was killed, not so much by the fact that *The Beggar's Opera* made its conventions ridiculous (for its conventions could at that time have been ridiculous only to quite unmusical people), as by the incontestable attraction of the new work itself. It was witty and outspoken, with abundance of topical satire; its music consisted of the tunes that everybody knew, and it presented the public with the irresistible fascinations of Lavinia Fenton, who was soon to become the Duchess of Bolton.

Handel may well have resented the success of *The Beggar's Opera*, but the collapse of the Academy was in reality no great disaster for his own interests. In the first place, he had done very well out of it from a financial point of view; the noble directors might have lost their money, but he had been only their paid servant, in which capacity he had accumulated enough to invest no less than £10,000 of his own in the next operatic venture. He obviously realised the strength of the position which he had built up for himself both as a composer and as a man of business. The most important result of the Academy's career had been to provide Handel with the opportunity of consolidating his own style as a composer of musical drama. Like all the court composers of his age he had provided whatever his patrons required—chamber music, water music, minuets for court balls, Church music for royal ceremonial; but the music on which his own heart was set was that of the theatre.

CHAPTER V

Handel had by this time definitely decided to make England his home; on February 13, 1726, he had been naturalised as an English subject. He had every reason to regard England as the best place in which to live. He enjoyed the protection of the German court; George II and Queen Caroline gave him indeed a good deal more encouragement than George I. The appointments of composer to the Chapel Royal and composer to the court were purely honorary, but they strengthened his position. As to the opera-house, he must by now have felt that he was its unquestioned autocrat, and he could not help being aware that he was without a rival in Europe as far as the stage was concerned, for old Scarlatti had gone to his grave, and the younger generation had produced no composer of such outstanding eminence. And in England music was generously rewarded from a material point of view; high fees were paid, not only to singers, but to teachers as well, and England was also one of the few countries where music-printing was a flourishing business. A good proportion of Handel's savings must have come from the sale of his published compositions; among Handel's contemporaries no other composer in Europe had so many of his works printed during his lifetime. English society seemed always ready to subscribe for a new musical work, and neither in Paris nor in Amsterdam was music so admirably engraved as in London.

Encouraged by the Princess Royal, Handel went into partnership with Heidegger, who had also made his own profits out of the opera, as well as out of his notorious masquerades; they leased the King's Theatre for a period of five years. The first thing to do was to secure new singers, and for this purpose Handel went to Italy, probably in the autumn of 1728. Heidegger had already tried to bring back Senesino and the two "costly canary-birds," as Colley Cibber called them, but they had had enough of London, and probably of Handel too. Little is known of the details of this Italian journey; it has been said that Handel travelled with Steffani, but this is impossible, as Steffani died at Frankfurt early in the year. Mainwaring tells us that, at Rome, Cardinal Colonna invited him to his palace, but that Handel, hearing that the Pretender was staying there, prudently declined the invitation. In engaging singers he seems to have been perhaps more prudent than was desirable, for his new company did not contain any very distinguished names. In place of Senesino he obtained the *castrato* Bernacchi; his new first woman was Signora Strada del Po', who was a fine singer, but so unattractive in appearance that London nicknamed her "The Pig." It is interesting to note that he also engaged a tenor, Annibale Fabri, although in those; days tenors were considered only fit for old men's parts of minor importance, and at Naples were generally given the parts of comic old women. Fabri's wife and another woman were announced as good actresses of male parts. "Fabri has a tenor voice," wrote Mrs. Pendarves, "sweet, clear and firm, but not strong enough, I doubt, for the stage. He sings like a gentleman, without making faces, and his manner is particularly agreeable." Perhaps Handel's friendship with Mrs. Pendarves had given him a sure insight into the taste of English gentlewomen.

In the summer of 1729 Handel paid a visit to his mother at Halle; she was then blind and half paralysed. Bach sent his son Friedemann over from Leipzig to beg Handel to come and see him, as he was himself too ill to make the journey, but Handel not unnaturally declined. Towards the end of June he passed through Hanover, and also went to Hamburg, where he engaged a German bass Riemschneider.

The opera season began on December 2, with Handel's *Lothario*, but it had only a moderate success. After a few revivals of *Giulio Cesare*, he brought out a second new opera, *Partenope*, on February 24. Despite its many beauties, it was even less successful than *Lothario*. Handel's audience did not go to the theatre to listen to his music; they went to hear the singers, and Bernacchi, who was no longer a young man, was a poor substitute for Senesino. Strada was the only member of the company who interested the audience. For the next season something better had to be found, and through Francis Colman, the English Envoy at Florence, Senesino was persuaded to accept 1,400 guineas instead of the 2,000 that he had received before. He opened the season of 1730 on November 3, with his former rôle of Scipio. For the moment Handel remained in the background; the next opera was a *pasticcio*, that is, an opera made up of favourite songs from various operas stuck into any convenient libretto. On February 2 there came out the new opera of Handel, *Poro*, which turned the tide once more in the composer's favour. Later on, *Rinaldo* and *Rodelinda* were revived, but the season came to an early end on May 29. For the following winter some changes were made in the cast. Senesino and Strada were of course indispensable, and the most important new acquisition was Montagnana, the bass, for whom Handel was to write some of his most celebrated songs.

After revivals of *Tamerlano* and *Admeto*, Handel brought out *Ezio* on January 15, 1732; it had only five performances. *Sosarme* (February 19) had ten; it is remembered now by the exquisite song, "Rendi 'l sereno al ciglio," which was sung by Strada. The remainder of the season presented nothing of any special interest until on the last night Handel offered his subscribers a new type of entertainment in the shape of *Acis and Galatea*.

On Handel's birthday, February 23, Bernard Gates, the master of the children of the Chapel Royal, arranged a private performance of *Esther*, which had been neglected since its first performance at Canons some twelve years before. Among the boys who sang and acted in the "masque" were Beard, who afterwards became Handel's favourite tenor, and Randall, eventually Professor of Music in Cambridge, who took the part of Esther. The performance was repeated twice before a paying public at the Crown and Anchor Tavern, where concerts were often held, and on April 20 a rival organisation advertised a further performance of Esther at the concert-room in Villiers Street. On this occasion it was described as "an oratorio or sacred drama," and was evidently sung without action. Princess Anne wished to see it on the stage of the opera-house but the Bishop of London forbade a dramatic performance. As the bishop's ban was ultimately the cause of Handel's turning his attention to oratorio in preference to opera, it has sometimes been suggested that Handel might have created a new type of national English opera on biblical subjects if only his lordship had not interfered. In justice to the bishop it has to be pointed out that his objection seems to have been raised, not against the dramatic presentation of Bible stories (for he did not discountenance Gates' performances by the choristers at the Crown and Anchor), but against their presentation in a regular theatre by professional opera singers. Such prejudice may be difficult to understand at the present day, but even well into the middle of the nineteenth century persons of severe morality regarded the theatre and all who belonged thereto with stern disapproval, and the notorious scandals associated with Cuzzoni and Faustina, to say nothing of Heidegger, were not likely to have washed out the memory of Jeremy Collier's denunciations.

"The sacred story of *Esther*, an oratorio in English," was accordingly announced for May 2, with the information that "there will be no acting on the stage, but the house will be fitted up in a decent manner for the audience; the Musick [i.e. the orchestra] to be disposed after the manner of the coronation service." Within a fortnight, Thomas Arne, father of the composer, advertised a performance of *Acis and Galatea* at the Little Theatre in the Haymarket "with all the choruses, scenes, machines, and other decorations, being the first time it was performed in a theatrical way." The laws of the time gave no protection to musical and dramatic copyright. Handel could only reply by giving a performance of the work himself; his one advantage was that as composer he could remodel the score and make several new additions to it. But he did not have the work acted; it was sung in costume with a background of appropriate scenery. Even in this form it obtained four performances; Senesino and Strada took part in it, singing in English.

Such a setting may appear strange to modern readers, but, even if it was a new idea for England at the time, it was a fairly well established tradition on the Continent, and Handel may very likely have seen a similar entertainment in Italy. The subscribers to the opera would see little in it that was incongruous. They were accustomed to see singers in all operas wearing dresses that differed very little from their own, and scenery which recalled their own Italianate gardens and palaces; Handelian opera, in any case, left little scope for what most people now call acting. At the same time we may be pretty sure that concert singers, especially Italians, allowed themselves far more liberty of spontaneous expressive movement than Victorian oratorio singers holding their music-books in front of them by traditional convention.

Four more performances of *Acis and Galatea* were given at the opera-house in December 1732; Handel evidently saw that it would be a sure attraction. *Alessandro* and *Tolomeo* were revived, and on January 23 he produced a new opera, *Orlando*, which had ten performances, with six more later in the season. *Orlando* is one of Handel's most original operas; he seems always to have derived a peculiar inspiration from the poems of Tasso and Ariosto, as in the case of *Rinaldo*. *Orlando* is a thoroughly romantic opera—Chrysander even compares it with those of Weber—full of episodes of madness and magic; it is so far removed from the ordinary conventions of its time that we can well imagine it to have startled both its audiences and its singers.

The affairs of the opera-house were going badly, and it is probable that there were considerable dissension within its walls. It is certain that relations between Handel and Senesino were becoming more and more strained; *Orlando* was the last opera of Handel's in which he sang. It seems fairly certain also that Heidegger was none too loyal as a partner. Heidegger was in a strong position, for he was the actual owner of the stock of scenery and other appurtenances taken over from the original Academy. He seems to have lent the theatre to Buononcini for some performances of *Griselda*, and, when the lease came to an end, it was Heidegger who left Handel in the lurch and allowed a rival organisation to secure it.

There was, too, a further reason for the general hostility against Handel. Encouraged by the success of *Acis and Galatea*, he had composed a new oratorio, *Deborah*, which was performed at the opera-house on March 17, by the King's command. For this work prices were doubled; tickets were a guinea each, and admission to the gallery half a guinea, instead of five shillings. At the second performance the normal prices were charged. The raising of prices for an extraordinary performance might well seem nothing unreasonable; but the event came exactly at the moment of the popular outcry against Walpole's Excise Bill, and the satirists of the day seized the opportunity of comparing Handel with Walpole.

Handel was now nearly fifty years of age. In the days of *Rinaldo* he had been a young man of twenty-five, making friends with those of his own age or younger, a new attraction with all the fascination of genius and youth. In the course of a generation he had become an established institution. He had made a success; he had amassed a fortune; he had secured to himself the unshaken confidence of the court; but he had inevitably made enemies. The native musicians were very naturally jealous of the foreigner, and the numerous foreign musicians in London jealous of one who made more money out of the extravagant English than they did themselves. The Italian singers found him tyrannical, and society very probably resented his rough manners. Society had engaged him to provide music for their entertainment, and he took up the unheard-of attitude of expecting society to pay its guineas for whatever music he chose to write. England, one might almost say, had spoiled him, for it was only in England that "The Great Bear," as he was sometimes called, could go his own way—a musician behaving with the complete disregard of public opinion which was considered the exclusive privilege of the English nobility. In any other country he would have been forced either to pander to the taste of a court or to relapse into obscurity. It was not until after the French Revolution that a Beethoven could display the independence of Handel in the aristocratic environment of Vienna.

The English nobility, having set Handel this example, claimed their own rights, and organised a rival opera-house at Lincoln's Inn Fields. They had no difficulty in seducing, first Senesino, then Montagnana, and finally Heidegger. Only Strada remained faithful to Handel. Buononcini having lost their favour, they engaged as composer the Neapolitan Nicolo Porpora, famous then as a great trainer of singers, and still more famous in later years as the teacher of Haydn. If Handel had the King and Queen on his side, the nobility could count on the support of Frederick Prince of Wales, who was immensely popular throughout the country and was on the worst possible terms with his royal parents. The Opera of the Nobility, as the new syndicate was called, was making its plans in good time, directly after the end of Handel's season.

In July 1733, Handel was invited to Oxford for a series of performances of his works, and it was proposed to confer on him the honorary degree of

Doctor of Music. The Vice-Chancellor, Dr. Holmes, was a loyal Hanoverian, and hoped by honouring Handel to do something to counteract the Jacobite reputation of the University. *Esther* and *Deborah* were performed, as well as the Utrecht *Te Deum* and *Jubilate*, and the Coronation Anthems; Handel further provided a new oratorio, *Athaliah*. The degree he refused to accept, for what reason has never been explained. Various suggestions have been offered. The Abbé Prevost, who was in England at the time, says that he refused the degree out of modesty; later biographers have differed in their views as to whether modesty was one of Handel's characteristics. Others have supposed that he refused to pay the fee of £100 that was demanded, but it is inconceivable that a fee should have been demanded for an honorary degree, although it would naturally have been paid by candidates who took the degree in the normal way. The concerts were attended by large audiences, many music lovers coming over from Eton and Cambridge, although there was considerable resentment at the price of admission—five shillings, a small amount compared with Handel's London charges. This "Handel Festival" at Oxford is significant, for it shows that in the space of no more than a year oratorio had begun to make a wide appeal, even outside London, although it was a form of composition that was new to English audiences. *Esther*, considered as a masque to be acted, might be said to continue the English traditions of the previous century, but there was no precedent in England for anything like *Esther* in concert form. The only English works which offered anything remotely like oratorio were the odes of Purcell and Blow for the musicians' festivals on St. Cecilia's Day, apart from the greater services and anthems of Purcell, which were composed, not for entertainment, but for liturgical use.

After the Oxford concerts, Handel and Schmidt went to Italy to look for singers. They heard Farinelli, the most famous *castrato* of the century, but did not engage him; perhaps his demands were too high. The *castrato* whom they did engage was Carestini, who, though less celebrated, was at any rate a singularly artistic singer. Durastanti came back, and, in place of Montagnana, Handel contented himself with Waltz, a German, who is often described as having been Handel's cook. Burney, at any rate, recorded that he was said to have filled this office, but Burney remembered him chiefly as a popular comic singer. He had sung Polyphemus in Arne's pirated performance of *Acis and Galatea*, and owing to the defection of Montagnana, took his place in *Athaliah* at Oxford. He had "a coarse figure and a still coarser voice" (Burney).

Handel opened his season on October 30, 1733. He had already finished the composition of a new opera, *Ariadne*, but it was not brought out until January 26, 1734. The reason, no doubt, was that an opera on the same subject by Porpora was produced by the Opera of the Nobility on December 29. Handel would no doubt have heard that it was in rehearsal, and have postponed his own production until he could see how Porpora's was succeeding. The two operas obtained the same number of performances, but Handel's theatre was seldom full, and many opera-goers were dissatisfied at his giving them oratorios, such as *Deborah* and *Acis*, on opera nights; these, however, seem to have been commanded by the King, and that in itself would make them all the more unpopular.

In March the Princess Royal was married to the Prince of Orange, and Handel was commissioned to write a wedding anthem. He also provided a secular entertainment in the shape of *Parnaso in festa*, described as a *serenata*. It was not unlike a masque; Apollo and the Muses appeared in costume on Mount Parnassus, but apparently there was no acting. The music was adapted from *Athaliah*, which, so far, had only been heard at Oxford. Oratorio was also attempted by Handel's rival; Mrs. Pendarves heard a work of his at Lincoln's Inn Fields in March. "It is a fine solemn piece of music," she wrote, "but I confess I think the subject too solemn for a theatre. To have words of piety made use of only to introduce good music, is reversing what it ought to be, and most of the people that hear the oratorio make no reflection on the meaning of the words, though God is addressed in the most solemn manner." Needless to say, it was "not equal to Mr. Handel's oratorio of Esther or Deborah." Mrs. Pendarves was at this time a near neighbour of Handel's in Lower Brook Street; one of her letters describes a small musical party (her musical parties were always small) a month later. Apparently there were not more than ten guests, including Lord Shaftesbury, who begged another guest to bring him, and was admitted as being "a profess'd friend of Mr. Handel"; the only professional musicians present were Handel and Strada. "I never was so well entertained at an opera! Mr. Handel was in the best humour in the world, and played lessons and accompanied Strada and all the ladies that sung from seven o' the clock till eleven." In such company Handel could evidently be more agreeable than on the stage at rehearsals, and it is interesting to note that the amateurs had no timidity about singing before Strada, and that Handel was willing to accompany all of them alike.

In July 1734, Handel's lease of the King's Theatre came to an end, and he found the theatre let at once by some means to his rivals, the Opera of the Nobility. He therefore entered into an arrangement with Rich for the use of his new theatre in Covent Garden, but his autumn season actually opened at Lincoln's Inn Fields on October 5. The probable reason for this was that the Princess Anne was spending the summer in England and wished to hear some of Handel's operas. She was a remarkably gifted musician, and Handel considered her to be the best of his pupils; she not only sang and played the harpsichord well, but was thoroughly grounded in the theoretical side of music and quite capable of composing a fugue, according to a Dutch musician who became acquainted with her after her marriage. She came to England on July 2 for a long stay, and at once persuaded Handel to give three additional performances of *Il Pastor Fido*, which he had revived that season. *Pastor Fido* and *Ariadne* were given again for her in October; probably Covent Garden was not quite ready for performances. Princess Anne left England on October 21, and her last words at parting were to beg Lord Hervey to do all he could to help Handel.

The chief attraction to the public at Covent Garden was probably not Handel but Mlle Sallé, a French dancer who had been engaged by Rich. The first performance at the new theatre was a ballet, *Terpsichore*, in order that she might inaugurate the season. *Terpsichore*, which includes songs and a chorus, served as prologue to *Il Pastor Fido*. The next opera was *Oreste, a pasticcio* made up by Handel himself from his own works; on January 8, 1735, he produced his Ariodante, an opera over which he had spent the unusually long time of ten weeks. The score was begun on August 12 and finished on October 24. The story is taken from Ariosto, and, as with Orlando, Handel found that it afforded opportunities for his peculiar vein of romanticism. On April 16 he followed it up with Alcina, again on a subject from Ariosto, and one of even more romantic character. Ariosto's enchantress Alcina was the model for Tasso's better-known Armida, who provided both Lulli and Gluck with one of their most dramatic heroines, and Burney says, with some justice, that Handel's Alcina gave birth to all the Armidas and Rinaldos of modern times. Both Ariodante and Alcina contained a large amount of ballet music, and the dances in Alcina, intermingled with choruses in the French manner, are among Handel's most attractive compositions.

Mrs. Pendarves, after the rehearsal of Alcina, described Handel as himself "a necromancer in the midst of his own enchantments," but he could not prevail against the enchantments of Farinelli, who had been engaged by the rival opera company. There could be no competing against a combination that included along with him Senesino, Cuzzoni, and Montagnana. The one powerful counter-attraction that Handel could offer was oratorio on Wednesdays and Fridays in Lent, when operas were not allowed to be given. Porpora's David, which the rival management put on, had no chance against Esther, Deborah, and Athaliah. Alcina carried the Opera on to the end of the season, the well-known air "Verdi prati," which Carestini had at first refused to sing, being encored at every performance. Handel's alleged angry retort to Carestini in comical broken English has been often quoted from Burney; but Schoelcher very sensibly observed that Handel was pretty certain to have conversed with Carestini in Italian.

The newspapers informed the world in May that Handel was going to spend the summer in Germany. His health had been seriously undermined, and it may well have been possible that he had talked of taking a cure at Aix-la-Chapelle; but on this occasion he went no farther than Tunbridge Wells. It was probably in the earlier part of 1735 that he made the acquaintance of Charles Jennens, a young man who was eventually to play a great part in his life, for on July 28 he wrote to Jennens to say that he was just starting for Tunbridge.

The letter is so short that it may be quoted here in full, for it gives us a great deal of interesting information.

London,

July 28, 1735.

Sir,

I received your very agreeable letter with
the enclosed Oratorio. I am just going to Tunbridge;
yet what I could read of it in haste,
gave me a great deal of satisfaction. I shall
have more leisure time there to read it with all
the attention it deserves.

There is no certainty of any Scheme for
next Season, but it is probable that something
or other may be done, of which I shall take
the liberty to give you notice, being extremely
obliged to you for the generous concern you
show upon this account.

The Opera of Alcina is a writing out, and
shall be sent according to your direction. It is
always a great pleasure to me if I have an
opportunity to show the sincere respect with
which I have the honour to be,

Sir,

&c., &c.,

GEORGE FRIDERIC HANDEL.

Jennens was a conspicuous figure in the London society of his day. At the time of this correspondence he was thirty-five, and unmarried; he had inherited vast wealth in his youth and spent it freely. He was ostentatious, even for an age when extravagance was fashionable; but although he was conceited and on occasions foolish, he was certainly possessed of considerable intellectual gifts, and the things which interested him most in life were literature, music, and the fine arts. The letter shows us that he must have admired *Alcina* sufficiently to ask the composer for a copy of the score. He also seized the opportunity of offering him a libretto for a new oratorio. He had a very good opinion of himself as a poet, and it is possible that he foresaw the importance of the new type of semi-dramatic entertainment which Handel was creating. There were plenty of Italian poetasters, even in London itself, who could put together a conventional opera-book, but English oratorio was still in the making, and it was not so easy to find a literary framework for it.

In any case, it was evident that Italian opera was a precarious enterprise. In October the papers again gave out that Handel was going to give oratorios and concerts at Covent Garden; no operas were announced, and for the time being Handel appeared to have abandoned opera altogether. He made no move until Lent 1736, and then brought out *Alexander's Feast* (February 19), which he had set to music in the previous two months. Those ever popular favourites *Esther* and *Acis and Galatea* followed it, and, as in the foregoing season, Handel played organ concertos between the acts of these works. It is evident that as Handel could not secure the great Italian singers for his oratorios he felt obliged to offer his public some other display of virtuosity, and his own performance on the organ seems to have been considered a very powerful attraction.

The marriage of the Prince of Wales to Princess Augusta of Saxe-Gotha (April 27, 1736) provided him with unexpected opportunities for coming before the public. It seems to have been at the desire of the Princess herself that he undertook a short Italian opera season of eight performances, which eventually was extended to ten. *Atalanta*, Handel's new opera for this season, in which the chief singer was Gizziello, then making his first appearance in England, was composed especially to celebrate the royal nuptials, and seems to have finally converted the Prince of Wales to the music of Handel. He now became a regular supporter of Handel's theatre, with the result that the King promptly withdrew his patronage, as he refused to be seen in the same house as the Prince. Encouraged by this sign of princely favour, Handel reopened Covent Garden in November with a revival of *Alcina*, followed by

Atalanta. Three more new operas were ready, or nearly so; Handel seems to have prepared himself for the winter in better time than usual. But neither *Arminio* (January 12, 1737), nor *Giustino* (February 16), nor even *Berenice*, with its famous minuet (May 18), could save Handel from ruin. The rival opera-house was in no better case. Handel was obliged to close Covent Garden on June 1, and the Haymarket followed suit ten days later. Opera at both houses had been killed, mainly by the folly of party strife.

CHAPTER VI

The collapse of the Opera left Handel not only bankrupt, but with seriously endangered health. In April 1737 it had been announced that he was "indisposed with the rheumatism," from which he made a slight temporary recovery; but before the season was over it became clear that he was suffering from paralysis. "His right arm was become useless to him," says Mainwaring, "and how greatly his senses were disordered at intervals, for a long time, appeared from an hundred instances, which are better forgotten than recorded." With some difficulty his medical advisers persuaded him to go to the sulphur bath of Aix-la-Chapelle, where, according to Mainwaring, he submitted to prolonged and drastic treatment. His cure was considered remarkably rapid, and the nuns (presumably nursing sisters) who heard him play the organ within a few hours of leaving his bath ascribed it to a miracle. "Such a conclusion," observes our clerical biographer, "in such persons was natural enough."

It has been asserted that during his stay at Aix, Handel composed a cantata for the five-hundredth anniversary of the foundation of Elbing, a town in East Prussia between Danzig and Königsberg. A German researcher about 1869 appears to have discovered documents at Elbing mentioning the cantata, with the name of the poet and that of a local singer, Jean du Grain, who composed the recitatives; Handel "of London" was said to have composed the choruses. No trace of the music has survived, and there seems to be no evidence whatever to connect this work with Handel's visit to Aix. Nor is it possible to suggest any reason why the authorities of this remote place should have applied to Handel for a composition.

According to Mainwaring, Handel stayed six weeks at Aix; the London papers announced his return on November 7, 1737. The management of the Opera had now been taken over by Heidegger, but the death of Queen Caroline on November 20 caused all theatres to be closed from that date until the end of December. It was announced in the papers that the Opera would reopen on January 10 with a new oratorio by Handel, called *Saul*, but this performance did not take place, and the theatre actually reopened on January 7 with his new opera *Faramondo*. This opera was the first work that Handel had undertaken after his return to London, but its composition was interrupted by that of the Funeral Anthem for the Queen. Although she died on November 20, Handel did not receive the King's command to write the anthem until December 7, as George II was strangely undecided in making arrangements for the funeral. It was finally fixed for December 17, and a special organ was hurriedly built for it in Henry VII's chapel at Westminster Abbey. Handel's anthem was performed by 80 singers and 100 instrumentalists. Queen Caroline had been one of his most faithful friends, and his gratitude and affection for her found utterance in music which Burney placed "at the head of all his works for expression, harmony and pleasing effects."

It was at ten at night on Christmas Eve that Handel finished the score of *Faramondo*; on Boxing Day he began the composition of *Serse*. *Faramondo* had only six performances, and *Serse* did not appear on the stage until April 15, when it ran for five nights only. It is remembered now, if at all, by the fact that the first song in it is the so-called "celebrated Largo," but the opera as a whole is of curious interest. "He was neither in health, prosperity, or spirits," says Burney, "when it was composed; appearances remain in his foul score [i.e. rough copy] of a mind disturbed, if not diseased. There are more passages, and even whole pages, cancelled in this score, than in any one of all his former operas." *Serse*, it must be explained, is a comic opera, and the only comic opera that Handel ever wrote. What induced him to attempt this style it is difficult to conceive. It is of course true that the failure of Handel's earlier operas was largely due to the success of *The Beggar's Opera* (1728), and of other comic entertainments which succeeded it—*Hurlothrumbo* (1729), *Pasquin* (1736) and *The Dragon of Wantley* (1737). A new type of comic opera had arisen in Italy too, and comic *intermezzi* were first seen in Italian grand opera in London in January 1737, although it was not until 1748 that a real company of Italian comic-opera singers came over to England. But what is more important to notice is that the whole style of Italian opera was changing during the second quarter of the century. Handel had continued to develop his own style, based on the grand manner of old Scarlatti, but Handel's operas were practically unknown outside London and Hamburg; in Italy, Scarlatti's style had already become old-fashioned before his death in 1725, and opera was moving on towards the lighter and flimsier manner of Galuppi, who first came to London in this year of *Serse*, 1738.

In choosing the libretto of *Serse*, Handel seems to have been making a desperate attempt to keep up with the taste of the day. Humour he had in plenty; one has only to recall *Acis and Galatea*. But the humour of *Serse*, diverting as it is to the modern historical student, is neither the musical nor the dramatic humour of 1737; the plot bears no resemblance whatever to the Neapolitan comic operas of Vinci and Pergolesi, but rather recalls the very early operas, based on Spanish comedies, composed by Alessandro Scarlatti in the 1680's. *Serse* was revived a few years ago in Germany, considerably cut about and reduced to one act, in which arrangement it had some success; but we can well understand its complete failure on its first London production.

The only satisfaction which Handel received in that unfortunate season of 1738 was the proceeds of his benefit concert at the Haymarket on March 28, organised for him by his friends, apparently rather against his own wish. According to Burney the net receipts were £800; Mainwaring puts the figure at £1,500. Even if we accept Burney's estimate, the sum is remarkable, and particularly so in view of the known hostility of a large section of society towards the composer. It can only be supposed that Handel's physical and mental collapse had been grave enough to awaken a wide-spread sense of pity for his misfortunes. Another mark of popular appreciation was the erection of a statue of Handel, executed by Roubiliac, at Vauxhall Gardens, in recognition of the pleasure which his music had afforded to the frequenters of that famous resort. This piece of "laudable idolatry," as Burney calls it, was thus described by a contemporary journalist: "Mr. Handel is represented in a loose robe, sweeping the lyre, and listening to its sounds; which a little boy sculptured at his feet seems to be writing down on the back of a violon-cello. The whole composition is in an elegant taste." Commissioned by an impresario who had made a fortune out of the use of Handel's music, it now appropriately adorns the vestibule of Messrs. Novello's music-shop in Wardour Street.

Charles Jennens, writing to his cousin Lord Guernsey on September 19, 1738, remarks that "Mr. Handel's head is more full of maggots than ever." Towards the end of July he had begun the composition of *Saul*, for which Jennens had provided the libretto three years before. It is evident that Handel intended to startle his audiences with his new oratorio scheme. He had ordered a new organ for the theatre at a cost of £500, constructed so that he might have a better command of his performers, and he had also acquired another instrument, which Jennens calls a "Tubalcain"—in other words a set of bells played from a keyboard—which he intended to use in the scene in which the Israelites welcome David after his victory over the Philistines. It is curious that Handel should have dramatised the insanity of Saul just after he had himself recovered from mental derangement.

No sooner was *Saul* finished (September 27) than Handel, four days later, began the composition of *Israel in Egypt. Saul* was first performed on

January 16, 1739, and enjoyed a moderate success, but *Israel* (April 4) was a failure, even after it had been shortened and made more attractive by the insertion of Italian opera songs.

Israel in Egypt is the most conspicuous example of a strange and almost unaccountable habit which from about this period began to show itself in Handel's methods of composition—the incorporation of large quantities of music by other composers. Samuel Wesley was the first person to draw attention to this practice of Handel's, though only in a private letter of 1808. In 1831 Dr. Crotch, in his professorial lectures at Oxford, named no less than twenty-nine composers whom Handel had "quoted or copied." The researches of Chrysander, Dr. Max Seiffert, Ebenezer Prout, and Sedley Taylor eventually proved beyond dispute that not only *Israel*, but several other works of Handel were largely made up from the music of other men.

Chrysander maintained that Handel began appropriating other men's ideas as early as 1707, for not only *Rodrigo* and *Agrippina*, but also *La Resurrezione* and the *Laudate pueri* show obvious reminiscences of Keiser's opera *Octavia* (Hamburg, 1705). These were probably subconscious, like Handel's reminiscences of Scarlatti and others at this period; they need not be taken any more seriously than Schubert's frequent reminiscences of Beethoven. But in *Atalanta* (1736) and *Giustino* (1737), Prout discovered quotations and adaptations several bars long from a *Passion* by Graun, which is known to have been composed not many years before. Further fragments of this *Passion* were identified by Prout in *Alexander's Feast* and the *Wedding Anthem* (1736); *Saul*, like *Israel*, incorporates several movements from a *Te Deum* by Urio (*fl.* 1660). From this date onwards until the end of his career Handel systematically drew upon the works of other musicians.

There has been much controversy over this question, and many attempts have been made to explain away Handel's "borrowings" so as to leave no moral stain on his character, which indeed, by all contemporary accounts, was scrupulously upright. Sedley Taylor (1906) was certainly anxious to clear Handel's character, but still more concerned to arrive at the exact truth, and his method of presenting the evidence throws a new light on Handel's procedure. He showed that in most cases Handel made frequent alterations in the music which he utilised, almost as if Stradella (to cite one name out of many) had been a young pupil to whom he was giving a lesson in composition.

A careful study of these alterations suggests a reason for Handel's action which seems not to have occurred to any previous writer on the subject. No one seems to have noticed hitherto that Handel's "borrowings" begin in 1736 on a small scale, and become more frequent in 1737, after which they develop into a regular habit. It seems only natural therefore to connect them with Handel's mental collapse; it became acute in the spring of 1737, but it may well have been approaching in the previous year.

There is no need to go so far as to suggest that Handel suffered from moral insanity and was incapable of distinguishing between right and wrong; but it is quite conceivable that his paralytic stroke affected his brain in such a way that he may sometimes have had a difficulty in starting a composition. Biographers of Handel have more than once drawn attention to phases in which he seems to have suffered from the inability to make a definite decision. Indecision is a common symptom of overstrained nerves, and anyone who has attempted musical composition or taught it to students will understand the hesitation and uncertainty which often attends the first writing down of a musical theme, although, once the initial idea has been settled, the continuation and development of it may proceed without difficulty. Any musician who studies the examples printed by Sedley Taylor will at once exclaim that for a man of Handel's experience, to say nothing of his fertility or indeed of his genius, it would have been far less trouble to compose an original setting of given words than to adapt them so laboriously to music written by someone else for a totally different purpose. But after his attack of paralysis there may well have been occasional moments when Handel could not make up his mind to write down an idea of his own, but may very likely have found that when once he had an idea ready on paper before him, whether that of another composer or an old one of his own, he could then continue to compose, and often make alterations in the music under his eyes which transformed it from a commonplace into a masterpiece.

In the autumn of 1739 Handel transferred his concerts to the smaller theatre in Lincoln's Inn Fields, where at first there seemed some hope of success. On November 17 he produced his setting of Dryden's *Ode for St. Cecilia's Day*; it was repeated several times, *Alexander's Feast* and *Acis and Galatea* being added to the programmes. But a month later an exceptionally severe frost set in; the Thames was frozen over, and for two months it was useless to open the theatre, owing to the impossibility of warming it adequately. In February he produced *L'Allegro*, adapted by Charles Jennens from Milton's *L'Allegro* and *Il Penseroso*, to which Jennens had added a third part of his own, *Il Moderato*; but the public, whether from indifference to the work or from fear of the cold, refused to come to it. Handel was once more on the verge of ruin, but that did not prevent him from giving a performance of his two most popular works, *Acis* and *Alexander's Feast*, for the benefit of a new musical charity.

The charity in which Handel was so keenly interested had been founded in 1738 to assist impoverished musicians and their families; it still carries on its honourable work under the title of the Royal Society of Musicians of Great Britain.

The same year saw the inauguration of another charitable institution which owed much to the continued generosity of Handel, the Foundling Hospital. Like Hogarth, who was also a benefactor, Handel did not confine his support to an occasional gift, but took the warmest personal interest in the place, and eventually both he and Hogarth were made governors of it.

The managers of the Opera had found themselves quite unable to continue productions on the grand scale of former years. In the winter of 1739-40 there had been an insignificant season at Covent Garden; it seems to have been directed by the Italian composer Pescetti, who, in the following winter, started concerts at the Little Theatre in the Haymarket. Mrs. Pendarves, who during the last few years had not lived much in London, and had thus dropped out of Handel's life, wrote in November: "The concerts begin next Saturday at the Haymarket. Carestini sings, Pescetti composes; the house is made up into little boxes, like the playhouses abroad." Dr. Burney gives a comic account of the undertaking. "The opera, a tawdry, expensive and meretricious lady, who had been accustomed to high keeping, was now reduced to a very humble state. Her establishment was not only diminished, but her servants reduced to half-pay. Pescetti seems to have been her prime minister, Carestini her head man, the Muscovita her favourite woman, and Andreoni a servant for all work." Concerts and *pasticcios* formed the main repertory, and Burney ascribes such success as they enjoyed to the fact that the Little Theatre was a "snug retreat" in which those who had the courage to quit their firesides during the great frost might keep reasonably warm.

Handel had nothing to do with this theatre, but in 1740 again rented the theatre in Lincoln's Inn Fields, where on November 8 he revived *Parnaso in Festa* "in its original oratorio manner, with the addition of scenes, dresses and concertos on the organ and several other instruments." It had but one performance; on the 22nd, Handel produced a new opera, or, as Burney calls it, an *operetta*, which had no more than two performances. This was *Imeneo*. On January 10, 1741, he brought out another new opera, *Deidamia*, which ran for three nights. *Imeneo* is a work of little importance; *Deidamia*, on the other hand, contains several very beautiful songs. But Dr. Burney, notwithstanding his admiration of it, has to admit that much of it was old-fashioned, in the style of Handel's youth, and sometimes "languid and antique." To Handel's admirers to-day such criticism may seem ridiculous, but to his audiences of 1741 these reversions to an earlier style would certainly have been most unwelcome.

Deidamia was Handel's last work for the stage; the glorious achievements of his youth and maturity had come to a hopeless end. His own public had unjustly neglected him, posterity consigned his operas to oblivion.

At some period during the summer of 1741 Handel received an invitation from the fourth Duke of Devonshire, then Lord-Lieutenant of Ireland, to go over to Dublin and give concerts there for the benefit of the local hospitals. It is very probable that Mrs. Pendarves may have helped to secure this engagement for Handel. She had spent a year and a half in Ireland in 1731-32, and her letters give a lively account of society in Dublin. Matthew Dubourg, an excellent violinist, was at the head of the Viceroy's band, and musical entertainments were frequent, for to judge from Mrs. Pendarves' descriptions the Irish bishops and deans lived almost as magnificently as the cardinals in Rome. Mrs. Pendarves was naturally a very popular guest in Dublin society; she was a remarkably fine harpsichord player for an amateur, and was constantly in demand as a performer at private parties. There was no one in London or Dublin who had a more intelligent understanding of Handel's music, and her enthusiasm for his works was unbounded. She kept constantly in touch with Dublin life when in England, for she corresponded with Dean Swift, and, what was more important still, she had in 1730 made the acquaintance of Dr. Delany, an Irish clergyman, whom she was to marry in 1743.

Handel did not leave London until the first week of November. During the summer he had been occupied with the composition of a new oratorio, *Messiah*, the words for which had been chosen and arranged by Jennens, apparently with a good deal of assistance from his chaplain, the Rev. Mr. Pooley. Whether *Messiah* was composed with a view to production in Dublin is not known; it was begun on August 22 and finished on September 14. A fortnight later he had completed the first act of *Samson*. On the way to Holyhead he stopped at Chester, where he was obliged to stay several days on account of contrary winds which prevented his embarking. He seized the opportunity to try over some of the choruses of *Messiah* with local church-singers, and Burney, who was at school at Chester, gives an amusing account of the little rehearsal, at which Handel was roused to grotesque fury by the inability of the bass, a printer by trade, to read "And with His stripes" at sight. On November 18 he arrived in Dublin, and opened his season at Neal's new music-hall in Fishamble Street on December 23 with a performance of *L'Allegro*, interspersed with concertos. A few days later he wrote a long letter to Jennens describing the unprecedented success which he had enjoyed. Dublin received him with open arms, and he thoroughly enjoyed his triumph, the more so as he felt himself to be in unusually good health.

A series of concerts followed, at which various oratorios and other works were performed. On April 8, 1742, there was a rehearsal of *Messiah*, open to those who had taken tickets for the first performance, which took place on Tuesday, April 13. The choir was provided by the singers from the two cathedrals, some of whom took the male solo parts as well; the female soloists were Mrs. Cibber and Signora Avolio. Over seven hundred persons were present, and about £400 was divided between the three charities, the Relief of Prisoners, Mercer's Hospital, and the Charitable Infirmary.

Saul was performed on May 25, and a second performance of *Messiah* took place on June 3. Handel left Ireland on August 13. In another letter to Jennens he says that his plans for the winter are undecided; for "this time twelve-month" (i.e. September 1743) he intended to continue his oratorios in Ireland. For some reason or other this second visit to Ireland never took place.

It was not until February 17, 1743, that Handel came before the London public again with *Samson*, which, unlike most of his oratorios, had an immediate success. He had by this time dropped the Italian singers altogether, and depended mainly on Mrs. Cibber and John Beard, a tenor who had more sense of artistic style than power of voice. Mr. Flower says that his voice was more powerful than sweet; Horace Walpole, who heard him, said that he had only one note in it, and Mrs. Pendarves, whose judgment was probably more trustworthy, said that he had no voice at all. The first London performance of *Messiah* was given on March 23, but it had no more than two subsequent repetitions this season. There were many reasons why it should have fallen flat. Jennens himself was extremely dissatisfied with it. *Israel* had been a failure too, and it is extremely probable that musical people, accustomed to the Italian opera, were estranged by a setting of Bible words in prose instead of a libretto in verse laid out on more or less dramatic lines.

William Law's *Serious Call* had been published in 1729; the book makes frequent allusions to the frivolity of Italian opera, and opera-going is picked out as one of the chief characteristics of irreligious persons. In 1739 John Wesley first began to preach in the open air; in 1742 Edward Young's *Night Thoughts* achieved its extraordinary popularity. These three events were all significant of the religious movement that was taking place among the more cultured classes in England, and this movement undoubtedly affected Handel's oratorio concerts. The ultra-religious were shocked at the association of sacred subjects with the theatre; those who could combine religion with culture, like Mrs. Delany, who was now approaching the age of piety, were Handel's most earnest supporters. It is quite probable that the section of society which preferred its culture unmixed with religion resented the attitude of the second party even more than that of the first, because the second party belonged to their own social class, and this resentment may well have contributed to the ever-increasing hostility shown by many social leaders toward Handel. And Handel's personal oddities were becoming rapidly more acute, partly owing to increasing age, and still more owing to recurrences of paralysis and associated mental derangement. He had another attack in this very year—1743.

Messiah and *Samson* were composed at a more favourable moment, and show little use of borrowed material, except that *Messiah* incorporates some of Handel's own chamber duets, the melodies of which were more suitably illustrative of their original Italian words than of the sentences from Scripture to which he adapted them. But his next important work, the *Te Deum* in celebration of the victory at Dettingen (June 27), begun in July and performed on November 27, incorporates no less than nine movements from the Latin *Te Deum* by Urio already drawn upon for *Israel in Egypt*. Mrs. Delany "was all raptures," and thought it "excessively fine."

It is curious that, whereas the Dettingen *Te Deum* was largely based on borrowed material, Semele, composed in the previous month of June, should be, as far as is at present known, entirely original. The libretto had been written by Congreve in 1707 for an opera, and it was only natural that its theatrical sense and its literary grace and distinction should have inspired Handel to one of his loveliest works. Handel was never quite at home in the English language, but in his later years he seems to have developed a feeling for English poetry, more especially for that of approximately his own time. But *Semele* did not attract the opera audience; it became increasingly clear that the opera party would have nothing to do with Handel, and were in fact deliberately doing all they could to bring him to ruin. Mrs. Delany and a few other great ladies remained faithful, but they were in a small minority. It was evidently the younger generation who were in opposition; Mrs. Delany alludes to them as "the Goths—the fine ladies, the *petits maîtres* and the ignoramuses," and seemed surprised that they allowed the oratorio to be performed without making a disturbance. Mrs. Delany was settling down to being the wife of a dean.

Joseph (March 2, 1744) fared no better, and Handel himself "was mightily out of humour about it" at the rehearsals. The summer was devoted to the composition of *Belshazzar*, for which Jennens had supplied the libretto. The collaboration was not altogether happy, for although Jennens had considerable sense of the picturesque, and offered Handel opportunities for what may be called spectacular music on the grand scale, his literary style was pompous, rhetorical, and long-winded. Handel protested perpetually against the length of the work, for the Handelian style of composition naturally extended the prolixity of the words; Jennens greatly resented the musician's criticism, and insisted on printing the poem in full.

When the winter came, Handel produced nothing of importance until January 5, when he brought out *Hercules*, a secular oratorio which he had composed in the summer during intervals when *Belshazzar* had to be laid aside owing to Jennens' delays. *Belshazzar* was given on March 27. *Semele*, *Joseph*, and *Saul* were revived, but, whatever oratorio was given, the theatre was almost empty, and the season came to a premature end on April 23. Handel was again suffering from some form of illness, and was unable to take any part in the performances, although he was present at them. Lady Shaftesbury describes "the great, though unhappy, Handel, dejected, wan and dark, sitting by, not playing on, the harpsichord," and adds that "his light had been spent in being overplied in music's cause." Hawkins states definitely that Handel became blind in 1751, and this date has been generally accepted; Lady Shaftesbury's letter suggests that he was already blind, or partially so, as early as March 1745, unless the word "light" is to be taken as meaning the light of his reason. This interpretation, in fact, is confirmed by a later letter of Lord Shaftesbury in October, in which he says: "Poor Handel looks something better. I hope he will entirely recover in due time, though he has been a good deal disordered in the head." Another friend of Handel's, William Harris, met him in London, in August, when he seems at first not to have recognised Harris and to have behaved with some oddity; "he talked much of his precarious state of health, yet he looks well enough."

It has generally been stated that in 1745 Handel again became bankrupt, but Barclay Squire pointed out that his name does not occur in the official lists of bankrupts. It must be remembered that, however disastrous his opera or oratorio seasons were, he had always his permanent pension of £600 a year to fall back on, and Hawkins states that this pension, originally granted by Queen Anne and George I, was punctually paid throughout his life.

From the end of August, London was in a panic over the Jacobite rebellion under the Young Pretender, Charles Edward. The Opera remained closed on account of the prejudice against the Papist Italian singers; at the other theatres patriotism expressed itself in appropriate music. Purcell's "Genius of England" was sung at one, Arne's recently composed "Rule, Britannia" at another, and on November 14 a "Chorus Song, set by Mr. Handel for the *Gentlemen Volunteers* of the City of London," was sung by Mr. Lowe at Drury Lane. The words suggest that the anonymous author was familiar with the Epilogue to Purcell's *King Arthur*; Handel's music is neither in his own style nor in Purcell's, but resembles the poorest sort of

English patriotic song of the early eighteenth century. Patriotic poetry was well illustrated by an additional verse for "God Save the King" which was printed in this same month:

From France and Pretender

Great Britain defend her,

Foes let them fall;

From foreign slavery,

Priests and their knavery,

And Popish Reverie,

God save us all.

On December 6 the Pretender began his retreat from Derby, and panic was allayed. Handel seized the opportunity to compose and bring out his *Occasional Oratorio*, about half of which was taken from *Israel in Egypt*; it contains a well-known quotation of "Rule, Britannia," and the point of the quotation is made clearer when we know that it was one of the patriotic songs sung at the theatres during the period of panic.

The Duke of Cumberland's defeat of the Pretender at Culloden on April 16, 1746, finally disposed of the Jacobites, and Handel made a further contribution to the national rejoicings in "A Song on the Victory over the Rebels," which was printed in the *London Magazine* for July. The words were by John Lockman; the first and last verses are as follows:

From scourging rebellion and baffling proud France,

Crown'd with laurels behold British William advance:

His triumph to grace and distinguish the day,

The sun brighter shines and all nature's gay.

Ye warriors on whom we due honours bestow,

O think on the source whence our late evils flow;

Commanded by William, strike next at the Gaul,

And fix those in chains would Britain enthral.

In the same month Handel began the composition of a new oratorio in honour of the Duke; this was *Judas Maccabaeus*, for which he had discovered a new librettist, the Rev. Thomas Morell, formerly Fellow of King's College, Cambridge. Morell has given a lively account of his collaboration with the great man, whom he did not fear to criticise. Handel's retorts to him have been reproduced as if they were outbursts of righteous indignation against a snarling poetaster, but, in view of many other records of Handel's rough tongue and genial humour (in which he seems often to have resembled Brahms), we need not take them too seriously. It is quite clear that Morell was more amused than offended, and the fact that they continued to collaborate up to the end of Handel's career as a composer shows that they must have remained on completely friendly terms.

Morell, to judge from the contemporary portrait of him, must have been a rather comic little figure with a strong sense of humour. He was a scholar, and something of a musician too. The academic primness of his verses has endeared him to all lovers of Handel, and to no one more than Samuel Butler; they are always admirably suited to their purpose, neat and scholarly, concise and direct, with never a word too many. They run easily for a singer, and it is not improbable that Morell was acquainted with the works of that great model of all opera-poets, Metastasio, for his words, like Metastasio's, acquire an unexpected beauty when they are sung.

Handel must have felt himself fully restored to health in the summer of 1746, for *Judas*, which was written in five weeks, contains no "borrowings," apart from a few numbers added some ten years later and adapted from some of his early Italian opera songs. It was not performed until April 1, 1747.

CHAPTER VII

The new oratorio met with surprising success. In the first place, Handel had given up the subscription system, and opened the theatre to all comers. The relief produced by the victory of Culloden had no doubt encouraged the general public to spend more money on entertainments; the Duke of Cumberland was a popular hero, and, through the *Occasional Oratorio*, Handel's name had come to be associated with him. *Judas* was naturally patronised by the court and by the Duke himself, who had made a handsome present to Morell in recognition of his literary laurels. And a new class of enthusiasts appeared in the shape of the Jews, we are told, who were attracted by the glorification of a national hero of their own. We do not hear much of the Jewish community in London in the days of Handel, and it cannot have been a very large one, but they appear to have been worth Handel's consideration. It may be mentioned that Handel's early librettist in London, Nicolo Haym, must have been a Jew, to judge from his name. Handel, at any rate, was sufficiently impressed to ask Morell to find another Jewish subject for his next oratorio; this was *Alexander Balus*, produced the following year.

The Italian opera party had this year engaged Gluck as a composer, and he too celebrated the Duke of Cumberland's achievements with an opera, *La Caduta dei Giganti* (January 5), which was a complete failure. It must have been put together in a hurry, for all of the "favourite songs" in it, published by Walsh (and no other record of the music remains), were taken from earlier operas of Gluck's; in any case they are poor stuff, and from Burney's description of the singers it is no wonder that the opera had no success. Gluck called on Handel, who told someone that he knew no more of counterpoint than his cook. Gluck was just under thirty, Handel just over sixty, and one can understand Handel's attitude; in any case he gave him some plain and practical advice as to how to please an English audience, which was not much use to Gluck, as he never visited this country again. Handel was quite right in his criticism, for Gluck was always very clumsy in his technique; and, at any rate, Gluck found him friendly enough and spoke of him forty years later with the profoundest respect. It is probable that Gluck heard *Judas*, as he was still in London in April.

A significant indication of the new popularity which Handel had acquired was the production of a *pasticcio*, at the Italian Opera in November 1747, made up chiefly from the operas of Handel; but the experiment was not repeated. In the autumn of 1748 a company of Italian comic-opera singers came over to London; they brought an entirely new type of entertainment, and after their success Handelian opera was buried for ever.

Alexander Balus was not one of Handel's popular works; *Joshua* (March 23, 1748) is now pretty well forgotten, but was a great attraction when new, mainly because it contained "See the Conquering Hero," which was afterwards transferred to *Judas Maccabaeus*. "What the English like is something that they can beat time to," said Handel to Gluck. He agreed with Hawkins in not caring very much for it himself, but added, "you will live to see it a greater favourite with the people than my other fine things." *Joshua* contains two "borrowings," one from Handel's own opera *Riccardo*, and another from Gottlieb Muffat.

The productions of the next year (1749) were *Susanna* (February 10) and *Solomon* (March 17); it is not known who wrote their libretti, though *Solomon* has been tentatively ascribed to Morell. *Susanna* was remarkably successful, perhaps on account of its story, which has always been a favourite with the painters of the later Renaissance. One can understand Lady Shaftesbury's saying, "I believe it will not insinuate itself so much into my approbation as most of Handel's performances do, as it is in the light operatic style." *Solomon* was a complete contrast, with its magnificent scenes of oriental pageantry.

The Peace of Aix-la-Chapelle (October 1748) had no doubt contributed, as the victory of Culloden did, to make people more inclined to enjoy the pleasures of life, with beneficial results to the organisers of music and drama. The King ordered a grand celebration of the event to take place on April 27, 1749, and preparations for it were begun as early as the preceding November. The famous theatrical architect Servandoni was commissioned to design an elaborate entertainment of fireworks on a colossal scale to be let off in the Green Park, accompanied by the music of Handel. The Fireworks Music was scored for fifty-six wind instruments. A rehearsal of it (without fireworks) was held at Vauxhall Gardens a week before, at half a crown admission, and it is said to have been attended by a crowd of twelve thousand persons. At the actual performance the fireworks were a disastrous failure, owing to various accidents, but Handel's music, accompanied by the firing of ordnance, was the real event of the evening. A month later Handel repeated the music at the Foundling Hospital, along with selections from Solomon, and a new work, composed for the occasion, known as the Foundling Anthem. His next act of generosity was to present the hospital with an organ, which he inaugurated on May 1, 1750, with a performance of Messiah. Henceforth the performance of Messiah at the Foundling Hospital for the benefit of the institution became an annual event, and it was this charitable association which really secured the work its subsequent popularity.

Handel's next oratorio, Theodora (March 16, 1750), came out at a bad moment, for a series of earthquakes were being felt in London, with the result that many people took refuge in the country, and those who stayed behind were reluctant to go to the theatre. The blame for the neglect which has always overtaken Theodora has been very unjustly laid on Morell. Handel himself, remembering the successes of Judas and Susanna, observed to the poet, "The Jews will not come to it, because it is a Christian story; and the ladies will not come, because it is a virtuous one." Theodora was always Handel's favourite among his oratorios, and he considered the chorus, "He saw the Lovely Youth," to be far beyond anything in Messiah. None the less, the theatre was half empty when Theodora was given. "Never mind," said Handel, with grim humour, "the music will sound all the better."

An old acquaintance reappeared this year in London in the shape of Cuzzoni, who had continued her quarrelsome career at Venice, Vienna, and Stuttgart. An unsuccessful benefit concert was given for her, at which Giardini the violinist made his first appearance in London. Handel engaged her to sing in Messiah at the Foundling Hospital, but her voice was gone. She was arrested for debt and bailed out by the Prince of Wales; after a few years in Holland, where she was again in prison, she died in destitution at Bologna.

In the summer Handel went to Germany for the last time. Nothing is known of his movements there beyond the fact that on the journey out he met with a carriage accident between the Hague and Haarlem. He was seriously injured, but was stated in a London paper of August 21 to be out of danger. Nor is it known when he returned; we have no further news of him until in January he began work on Jephtha. Morell says that he himself wrote Jephtha in 1751, but, as Handel had completed the first act on February 2, it is probable that Morell, like Jennens, supplied him with the words in instalments.

The composition of the music suffered various interruptions owing to the failure of Handel's eyesight, and possibly to a return of mental disorder (Streatfeild). He was able to play the organ at the Foundling Hospital in May, and directly afterwards went for a short visit to Cheltenham, returning to London on June 13. He resumed work on Jephtha, and finished it on August 30. It was some time this year (the precise date is unknown) that he consulted Samuel Sharp, a surgeon of Guy's Hospital, who told him that he was suffering from gutta serena, and that freedom from pain in the visual organs was all that he had to hope for during the remainder of his days. It was a severe shock, especially to a man whose general physical and mental health was already undermined, and it is no wonder that Handel began to give way to periods of profound depression. The condition of Handel's eyes, and of his hand as well, may be clearly observed in the autograph of Jephtha, and it may be noted that here he again reverted to the process of "borrowing"—this time from five Masses by Habermann, a composer twenty years his junior, published in 1747.

It may well be asked how Handel acquired the original copies of all the works which he utilised in his later years, since it is obvious that they could not have been well known or easily available to musicians in England. A guess may be hazarded that he obtained them through his old friend Telemann at Hamburg. Telemann, it will be remembered, had been a close friend of Handel's during their student days at Halle; whether they met again in Germany after Handel had taken up his residence in London is not known, but it is quite probable. The fact remains that Handel was undoubtedly in friendly correspondence with Telemann in 1750, for in December of that year he wrote a long letter to him (in French) thanking him for a theoretical work. Telemann appears to have been a keen gardener, and had evidently asked Handel to send him some rare plants. Handel's reply suggests that he was not much interested in gardening himself, but was most anxious to do all he could to give Telemann pleasure.

Another letter (again in French) to Telemann, dated September 20, 1754, explains that Handel had set about procuring the plants when Captain Carsten of Hamburg, by whose ship he intended to send them, told him that Telemann was dead; but, after another voyage to Hamburg and back,

Carsten brought the news that Telemann was alive and in good health. He also brought a list of the rare plants desired, and Handel writes to say that he has obtained almost all of them, and will send them by Captain Carsten when he sails for Hamburg again in December.

It is true that there is no mention of any parcel of music in these letters, beyond Telemann's "System of Intervals," but they suggest that they were part of a longer correspondence. Telemann was keenly interested in contemporary music, as his correspondence with Graun shows; he also seems to have asked Graun to send him plants from Berlin. He is the most likely person to have sent musical works of interest to Handel; possibly they were sent on loan, and returned after Handel had made the extracts which are to be seen in the Fitzwilliam Museum at Cambridge.

Jephtha was produced on February 26, 1752. Handel's oratorios had by now become a lucrative undertaking, and it was characteristic of English audiences that they came in crowds to see Handel playing the organ in his blindness, and enjoy the luxury of tears when Beard sang "Total Eclipse!" Sharp, the oculist, recommended Handel to employ as his assistant John Stanley, who had been blind from early childhood and was a singularly accomplished organist. Handel burst out laughing. "Mr. Sharp, have you never read' the Scriptures? Do you not remember? If the blind lead the blind, they both fall into the ditch."

He underwent various operations, but derived only partial benefit from them. During these last years he led a very retired life, but he continued to play the organ at his oratorios, at first from memory, and later extemporising the solos in his concertos, which were always an integral feature of his concerts. The profits of these were enormous, and when he died in 1759 he left investments to the extent of 20,000. Composition naturally became a more difficult matter after blindness set in, but new songs were added to many of the oratorios, and in 1758 he made a complete revision of his old Italian cantata, Il Trionfo del Tempo. Morell translated it into English, and seventeen new numbers were added. Some of these were new, but many were adapted from other works of Handel's, chiefly from Parnasso in Festa, and there are also borrowings from Lotti and Graun. Two choruses by Graun had already been utilised in the revision of the Italian version which Handel brought out in 1737.

All this time John Christopher Schmidt, now known as Smith, had been his indispensable factotum. Smith made fair copies of his music, and managed his affairs for him, though Handel, almost up to the end, seems to have discussed his investments in person with his financial adviser, Mr. Gael Morris, in the City. Smith's son, who had come with his father to London as a child, had been educated under Handel's direction, and in 1754 became the first organist of the Foundling Hospital. In Handel's later years it was the son who assisted him at the performances of the oratorios and acted as his musical amanuensis. There is a curious story of a quarrel which took place at Tunbridge Wells, about four years before Handel's death, between the two old men. The cause of it is not known, but it is stated to have been quite trivial; old Smith left Handel abruptly, and Handel vowed he would never see him again. The son attempted to heal the breach and even went so far as to say that he would refuse to assist Handel at his concerts any more unless Handel restored to his father the legacy which after the quarrel he had intended to leave to the son; young Smith foresaw that he himself would be accused of having deliberately alienated the affections of Handel from his father in order to secure the money for himself.

Handel apparently yielded to some extent, but it is clear that he was not reconciled to old Smith for a long time. "About three weeks before his death," we are told, in Coxe's Anecdotes of Handel and Smith, published soon after young Smith's death, "Handel desired Smith junior to receive the sacrament with him. Smith asked him how he could communicate, when he was not at peace with the world and especially when he was at enmity with his former friend, who, though he might have offended him once, had been faithful and affectionate to him for thirty years." Handel was much affected by Smith's words, and the reconciliation took place. Religion had gained a strong hold upon Handel in his years of suffering; he spoke much to Hawkins and others of his delight in setting the Scriptures to music, and he was a regular worshipper at St. George's, Hanover Square.

His last appearance in public was at the performance of Messiah on April 6, 1759, but at the end of it he was seized with a fainting attack, took to his bed, and died during the night between the 13th and 14th of April. He was buried in Westminster Abbey on the evening of the 10th; the choirs of the Chapel Royal and St. Paul's joined the Abbey choir in singing the burial music of Dr. Croft, and it is said that three thousand people were present.

Handel's will, executed June 1, 1750, left the bulk of his fortune to his niece and goddaughter Johanna Friderica Floerken (nee Michaelsen) of Gotha; other relatives were also left legacies. To Christopher Smith (junior) he left 500, besides his large harpsichord, his chamber organ, his portrait by Denner, and his manuscripts. He had at one time thought of leaving the manuscripts to the University of Oxford, and, having already promised them to Smith, offered him a legacy of £3,000 if he would resign all claim to them. Smith refused, and also refused an offer of £2,000 made for them, after Handel's death, by Frederick the Great. He kept them until 1772, when he presented them to George III in return for a pension of £200 a year. But he did not hand over the whole of the manuscripts to the King, and a large collection of rough sketches and fragments was acquired by Lord Fitzwilliam, who bequeathed them to the University of Cambridge.

The foregoing pages will have shown how singularly few are the definite facts about Handel's life which can be ascertained with any degree of certainty. There are a number of portraits which give some idea of his outward appearance, but most of them represent him as a man of middle age, and the anecdotes of his life and habits recorded by various contemporaries belong mostly to the same period. It is almost impossible to form any idea of his private character and his inward personality. Biographers of musicians often attempt to deduce their characters from their musical works, but it need hardly be said that such a procedure is thoroughly unreliable.

Portraits are notoriously unsafe as guides to the interpretation of character, but if the miniature reproduced by Mr. Flower as having been painted in Rome is an authentic likeness of Handel as a young man and it certainly bears some resemblance to the portrait by Denner painted about 1736 or 1737—he must have been singularly attractive in those days. It cannot have been his musical abilities alone that won him the immediate friendship of Telemann at Halle and Mattheson at Hamburg; and, although he seems from his earliest days to have been ambitious and determined to make a career for himself, his contemporaries give the impression that he was retiring rather than self-assertive. In later life he was often described as bearish and rough-mannered, but this cannot have been the case in his youth, or he would never have achieved the position which he held in the most cultured and distinguished society of Rome and Naples. His visit to Italy must inevitably have been a wonderful education in the humanities, otherwise he could never have been received as he was on his first visit to London by the society which most nearly resembled that of his Italian friends and patrons.

Professional musicians, and especially those connected with the theatre, were regarded in England as being more or less disreputable, unless they held university degrees and posts of distinction. Handel moved among them in his professional life, as was only natural, but his more intimate friendships seem, throughout his career, to have been confined mainly to the innermost circle of the well-bred amateurs; we must not forget, however, that it was only persons of that class whose letters and memoirs have come down to us. Burney and Hawkins at any rate were well acquainted with the professional world, and their testimony tends to confirm that Handel stood more or less aloof from it. It was only in later life that he associated on terms of friendship with such a person as Mrs. Cibber, the singer. In an age when all opera-houses were, with some truth, regarded as centres of sexual promiscuity, it is indeed remarkable that not the least evidence exists, with one solitary exception, that Handel was ever even alleged to have had an illicit love-affair. Mr. Flower discovered a copy of Mainwaring's biography, with marginal notes said to be in the handwriting of George III, and there we read: "G. F. Handel was ever honest, nay excessively polite, but like all Men of Sense would talk all, and hear none, and scorned the advice of any but the Woman he loved, but his Amours were rather of short duration, always within the pale of his own profession." The *Anecdotes of Handel and Smith* mention two occasions on which he was said to have become engaged to be married, or nearly so, but the writer is so reticent that little faith can be placed in his statement, and in any case the *Anecdotes*, published in 1799, are not very reliable as far as Handel is concerned.

It is not difficult to understand that there were two Handels, one "excessively polite" (which, in the language of the eighteenth century, does not mean that he was servile and cringing, but simply that he behaved like a man of good breeding), as he appeared to such people as Mrs. Delany and the Harris family, and the other as he showed himself at rehearsals, or in the society of men friends of more or less his own standing—bluntly outspoken and perhaps at times inconsiderate. The hostility of a large number of social leaders may well have been aroused in the first instance by some careless harsh word.

"The figure of Handel was large," says Burney, "and he was somewhat corpulent and unwieldy in his motions; but his countenance, which I remember as perfectly as that of any man I saw but yesterday, was full of fire and dignity; and such as impressed ideas of superiority and genius. He was impetuous, rough, and peremptory in his manners and conversation, but totally devoid of ill-nature or malevolence; indeed there was an original humour and pleasantry in his most lively sallies of anger or impatience, which, with his broken English, were extremely risible. His natural propensity to wit and humour, and happy manner of relating common occurrences in an uncommon way, enabled him to throw persons and things into very ridiculous attitudes. Handel's general look was somewhat heavy and sour, but when he did smile, it was his sire the sun, bursting out of a black cloud. There was a sudden flash of intelligence, wit, and good humour, beaming in his countenance, which I hardly ever saw in any other."

Both Burney and Hawkins record that outside his profession he was said to be ignorant and dull, and the fact that they are at pains to defend him on this charge shows that there was apparent ground for it. Pepusch said of him that he was "a good practical musician," which is what one might well expect of Pepusch, whose devotion to antiquarian learning aroused the amusement rather than the admiration of his contemporaries. Handel was at any rate keenly interested in painting, like Corelli, and the third codicil to his will, dated August 4, 1757, mentions two landscapes by Rembrandt, one a view of the Rhine, which he bequeathed to one of the Granvilles from whom he had received both as a gift.

Another characteristic of Handel's for which his early biographers are hard put to find an excuse was his enormous appetite for food and drink, satirised by his once intimate friend the painter Goupy in a well-known print called "The Charming Brute," in which Handel is represented with the head of a pig, seated at an organ, with various comestibles disposed at his feet. In this connexion it may be noted that for all his gluttony Handel was never accused of drunkenness; if he exceeded in the pleasures of the table, it was as a gourmet and a connoisseur. Yet it is recorded that he never led an extravagant life, and apart from this particular weakness he lived as simply in the days of his wealth as in those of his poverty. Generosity to those in distress was at all times characteristic of him.

Although Handel became a naturalised British subject, none of his contemporaries would ever have dreamed of regarding him as an Englishman, or as a composer of English music. Burney's account of the commemoration festival of 1784 may be regarded as an official panegyric, but even in that he goes no further than to say that Handel, "though not a native of England, spent the greatest part of his life in the service of its inhabitants, improving our taste, and introducing among us so many species of musical excellence, that, during more than half a century, while sentiment, not fashion, guided our applause, we neither wanted nor wished for any other standard. Indeed, his works were so long the models of perfection in this country, that they may be said to have formed our national taste." In the pages which deal with the character of Handel as a composer, he says that he united "the depth and elaborate contrivance of his own country with Italian elegance and facility." Handel's music, he holds, was from the first congenial to the English temperament, but he never regards it as being at all English in style, though in other writings he naturally recognises the occasional indebtedness of Handel to the influence of Purcell. It was only in the nineteenth century that Handel came to be regarded as a national institution. His own country for the most part neglected his works; his operas were thought impossible to revive, and the oratorios were considered by most Germans as being "too English" —an opinion which the writer of this book frequently heard expressed in Germany some fifty years ago. Since 1920 there has been an astonishing revival of Handel in Germany, beginning with the restoration to the stage of his operas—the last works of his which most people would have thought suitable for presentation to modern audiences—and much energy has been expended by German critics on an attempt to demonstrate the essentially Germanic character both of Handel's music and of his personality.

The more closely we study Handel in relation to his own times, and in relation to the general history of music, the clearer it becomes that Goupy the caricaturist was only right when he put into Handel's mouth the words, "I am myself alone."

The foundation of Handel's musical style was Italian, and it was only natural that this should be the case, for, in his days, Italy dominated European music as she did European architecture. All music in the grand manner, except in France, was Italian in its tradition, and if ever there was a composer who illustrated the grand manner throughout his life, it was Handel. France had produced a grand manner of her own, though not without an initial impulse from Italy; in all other countries north of the Alps native music was only for the humbler classes of society. When Handel condescended to it, as he did in the political excitement of 1745, he deliberately adopted the musical style of a tavern song.

Handel's serious music was never written for popular audiences; in his later oratorios he sometimes admittedly wrote down to the taste of the middle classes, but we have the records of his conversations with Gluck, Hawkins, and others to prove how little respect he had for that taste. He composed for the needs of the moment, and not with a view to immortality, but he composed for a society which was cultured enough to desire, even in its entertainments, grace, dignity, and serenity.

If Handel's works have for later generations become a source of joy and delight to a very different social class, it is because they are the musical equivalents of those palaces and gardens of Handel's day which are now national monuments and open to all comers. We walk beneath their colonnades, peopling them in imagination with the gracious and stately figures of the past; and from the museum of memory there arise the unheard strains of Handel's music:

> *Hark! the heavenly sphere turns round,*
> *And silence now is drown'd,*
> *In ecstasy of sound!*
> *How on a sudden the still air is charm'd,*
> *As if all harmony were just alarm'd*
> *And every soul with transport fill'd!*

BIBLIOGRAPHY

Mainwaring, J.: *Memoirs of the Life of the Late G. F. Handel*. London. 1760.

Burney, Charles: *A General History of Music*. London. 1776-89.

Burney, Charles: *An Account of the Musical Performances in Westminster Abbey, etc.* London. 1785.

Hawkins, Sir John: *A General History of the Science and Practice of Music*. London. 1776.

Coxe, W.: *Anecdotes of G. F. Handel and Y. C. Smith*. London. 1799.

Schoelcher, Victor: *The Life of Handel*. London. 1857. The first attempt at a complete and documented biography.

Chrysander, Friedrich: *G. F. Händel*. Leipzig. 1858-67. This biography does not go beyond 1740, but it is the most valuable source for carefully documented facts.

Delany, Mary: *Autobiography and Correspondence of Mary Granville, Mrs. Delany*. Edited by Lady Llanover. London. 1861-62.

Taylor, Sedley: *The Indebtedness of Handel to Works by Other Composers*. Cambridge. 1906.

Robinson, Percy: *Handel and His Orbit*. London. 1908.

Streatfeild, R.A.: *Handel*. London. 1909. The best biography of Handel and critical study of his works in English.

Squire, W. Barclay: *Handel in 1745* (Riemann-Festschrift). Leipzig. 1909.

Rolland, Romain: *Haendel*. Paris. 1910.

Flower, Newman: *George Frideric Handel: His Personality and His Times*. London. 1923.

This book contains much new biographical matter. I have to thank Mr. Flower for kind permission to make use of his valuable discoveries.

Leichtentritt, Hugo: *Händel*. Stuttgart. 1924. Biography based mainly on Streatfeild; gives a detailed analysis of all Handel's works.

Young, Percy M.: *Handel*. London. 1947.